The River Runs Salt, Runs Sweet

The River Runs Salt, Runs Sweet

Runs Sweet

A Young Woman's Story of Love, Loss and Survival

JASMINA DERVISEVIC-CESIC

NSPYR

Charlottesville

Published in the United States by NSPYR LLC
Cover Photo by Dickie Morris
Cover Design by Albano Design & Dickie Morris
Author Photo by Leila Cesic
Maps by Dickie Morris
ISBN 978-1-939495-02-0 (print)
ISBN 978-1-939495-03-7 (eBook)
NSPYR.com

*This book is dedicated to the memory
of my brothers Tajib and Samir,
my husband Suljo
and all of the other Muslims from my hometown
who died in the war.*

Contents

Foreword by Jay Lavender

When my good friend, Col Randy Larsen, USAF (Ret.), called me a few years ago about a book he'd just finished reading, I could hear in his voice that he'd found something truly special. Upon reading Jasmina's powerful story for the first time, I agreed with Randy's assessment. Her memoir, published independently in 1994, was a perfect story for NSPYR, the start-up production & publishing company I co-founded to tell great inspiring stories.

Since first reading *The River Runs Salt, Runs Sweet*, I've been fortunate to travel to the Boston area a few times to spend time with Jasmina and hear her harrowing and uplifting memories firsthand. We partnered to acquire the rights to her book from the original publisher then revised the text, added photos and a new cover for this NSPYR Edition.

Any successful story has many parents, many of whom go unacknowledged. A special thank you goes to Joanna Vogel and Bruce Holland-Rogers who helped Jasmina get her inspiring story on the page twenty years ago. Without their efforts, I wouldn't have the honor of writing these words.

With your help, we hope to share Jasmina's wonderful book with a wider audience, grow her speaking career and bring her remarkable life story to the screen. In doing so, we aim to create joy that might offset some of the indescribable pain that so many endured during The Bosnian War. For there will always be war. But in the survivors' stories we can find lessons and inspiration to help us persevere when we encounter turbulent times of our own.

My life's better off having read Jasmina's story and subsequently getting to know her—I hope you have the opportunity to do both.

Jay Lavender
Charlottesville, Virginia
July 2014

Bosnia
1992-1993

Visoko
o

Visegrad
o

Sarajevo

Gorazde
o

Introduction: Why I Wrote This Book

When I first came to the United States as a Bosnian refugee in 1993, the most difficult thing for me to deal with was not learning a new language, even though that was a real challenge. In fact, it was a challenge made urgent by my desire to speak to Americans about the war. I wanted the citizens of my new home to understand what was happening in my native land and I wanted them to see that there were things they could do to make a difference. I certainly didn't want Americans to give in to pessimism and despair when they heard the news from Sarajevo. It was important that Americans felt courage and hope for Bosnia and that they communicated those feelings to their leaders.

So I spoke out in my new language. It was hard, even with my new American friends helping me. I have always been shy. If three years before, you had told me that in 1993 I would be standing in front of a room full of people delivering a speech in a new language, I'd have said you were crazy. But I did it. I felt compelled to do it.

As I say, though, dealing with a new language or even making speeches in it was not my greatest challenge. My greatest challenge was that some people in the audience, upon seeing my wounds and hearing my story, clearly felt sorry for me.

I know that such concern is an expression of compassion, but, pardon me, I hate it. I can't stand to be pitied. I certainly wasn't struggling with all these irregular English verbs so that I could stand in front of 200 people who would feel sorry for me.

That was the toughest thing about coming to America. At least in Bosnia, people had been through similar things themselves. They could see in my war wounds what I saw in them—the history of my struggle to get on with life in spite of everything. A struggle I was winning.

When I first started to work on this book, I thought only of writing the story for Bosnia's sake. I wanted to bear witness to what had happened to my country and to the people I loved and lost. But as I wrote, I came to understand that my story was about much more.

Everyone experiences loss.

Everyone, even in peacetime, loses loved ones. Everyone feels jostled or even violated by events beyond their control. Everyone suffers the losses of disillusionment and betrayal, sooner or later.

My losses happened to come all at once—personally, physically and emotionally. I lost some of my faith in humanity when I discovered that people who were your best friends one day could conspire to destroy you the next. And there were more losses beyond that. Ultimately, I lost almost everything that many of us would call a normal life.

Yet here I am, on the road back not only to a normal life, but perhaps a happy one. And never, not even in the Sarajevo hospital when the doctors thought that I wouldn't walk again, was I without something to sustain me.

As I thought about the things that kept me going in the worst of times, I began to understand that my story was about more than Bosnia. It was about how we manage to endure, to support one another and to recover from the most difficult of trials.

Of course, that really is the story of Bosnia. My country has borne the assault of what was once its own national army, been carved up by Chetnik extremists and starved of the means to defend itself by the governments of Europe and America. Just as parts of me are missing, parts of Bosnia are missing. Just as I have lost my loved ones, Bosnia has lost many thousands of hers. Yet Bosnia endures and Bosnians even hope that one day, Sarajevo and our other cities will be the kind of places they once were, where Muslims, Jews, Catholic Croats and Orthodox Serbs live next door to one another, go to school together and intermarry. That was once our normal life. It's what we hope to return to.

I must admit up front that this book won't answer all your questions about the war as there is so much about the conflict that still mystifies me. Though there were villages that were exclusively Muslim, Serb or Croat in Bosnia, all the cities of any size were tolerant and integrated. The stories we heard from our grandparents about what the Chetniks did to the Muslims during World War II were just that: stories. People my age really didn't think those events had any relevance in our time.

I still find it hard to understand that one of the boys who played on my brothers' soccer team died with a gun in his hands, fighting as a Chetnik for a Greater Serbia that would mean the extermination of many of his old high school friends. Did he always hate a portion of his classmates? Was he hiding his genocidal politics all those years or did he change overnight? I can't say. Perhaps I will never know.

What I do know is that we must go on, each of us, building our own normal lives and doing what we can to heal the world.

I know that some parts of my story will be difficult to read but I hope you will keep this in mind—if it is a story of despair, it is also a story of deliverance. There is a passage in the Koran that says:

> *Nor are the two bodies*
> *Of flowing water alike—*
> *The one palatable, sweet,*
> *And pleasant to drink,*
> *And the other, salt*
> *And bitter. Yet from each*
> *Kind of water do ye*
> *Eat flesh fresh and tender,*
> *And ye extract ornaments*
> *To wear; and thou seest*
> *The ships therein that plough*
> *The waves, that ye may*
> *Seek thus of the Bounty*
> *Of God that ye*
> *May be grateful.*

Both the salty currents and the sweet ones nourish us in some way. The worst adversities bring the bounties of hidden strength along with the surprise that even the worst tragedies in life are overcome in the same way that the minor ones are: one step at a time.

Jasmina Dervisevic
Boston, Massachusetts
1994

1

The River Runs Salt

October 1986

The Drina River in Visegrad, Bosnia

When I think of Visegrad, of how it was when I was fifteen, I keep returning to memories of the rivers. My town was bounded by rivers—the Rzav on one side of the valley, the colder and deeper Drina on the other.

I grew up swimming in the rivers. In summer, the banks of the Rzav were our beach, the place where young people went to hang out. At the end of summer, there were races across the Drina with medals for the winners. The whole town would turn out to cheer. And all year round, people in Visegrad gathered in the cafés to talk about life and each other. You could always go into one of the cafés, find people you knew and pass an hour talking to them. In Visegrad, it was hard to be lonely. Even if you didn't want to talk, you might sit and watch the water flow by, keeping company with the Drina.

But not all of my memories of the Drina are good ones.

One cold day in October, 1986, around four p.m., almost everyone in my family was home from school and work having lunch when my five-year-old brother, Dervis, rushed into the house. His face was red and he was excitely trying to tell us something but he didn't know quite what to say. "Mama, mama, look how cold it is outside! And Bojan is swimming!" Bojan was the younger brother of my friend, Dragana. He was my brother's age but he was a lot noisier than my brother, or any other little boy, for that matter. When he was in front of our building, even from inside the apartment you could hear him. But he always had a smile which made it easy to forgive him for being so loud.

Bojan's father had always been afraid for his son. Two times, Bojan had almost died. The first time, his father had almost killed him. It happened right in front of our building. His father was a bus driver and as he drove his bus up our street one day he saw a big cardboard box in the road. Just before the bus got to it, the box moved. Bojan's father stood on the brakes, got out and checked to see what was inside. He expected to find a stray dog. Instead, it was his son.

The second close call happened while Bojan and his father were fishing one day in a boat on the Drina. Bojan's father turned away for a moment and Bojan jumped over the other side. The Drina is big and the current is fast. If Bojan's father had not seen where his son had gone in, he might have lost sight of him as he sank. As it was, Bojan almost drowned.

In Bosnia, we always believed that tempting fate for a third time was unlucky.

So there was my brother trying to explain something about Bojan and we weren't understanding. "Dervis," my mother said, "Where is Bojan? What is he doing?"

"He is swimming, Mama! In the Drina! We were leaving the Sports Center to come home and he was on the side of the bridge. He fell in the river. It's cold and he's swimming!" My poor brother. He knew it wasn't a good idea to swim when it was so cold but he didn't understand how much trouble Bojan was really in. He didn't understand that his friend could die. He was still talking about swimming in the cold weather when we hurried out of the apartment.

We were at the bridge in moments. Nearly all of Visegrad was already there. I looked for Bojan on the surface of the river. He wasn't there but I saw his sister, Dragana, swimming against the current and looking for him.

Bojan's mother was there, too. "Dragana!" she called out. "There! Look there! You have to find him. He is still alive. Bojan, Bojan, my son, where are you?" And sometimes when she cried out, it was without words. Every time she cried out like that, wordlessly, with a mother's fear, the sound cut me like a knife.

Dragana shouted, "I can't find him! Bojan! Bojan!"

It had already been quite some time since Bojan had disappeared. From the shore, people called advice to Dragana and her mother—look here, tell her to try over there, dive deeper. But nobody was jumping into the river to help. They were all afraid to because the Drina was so cold in October.

"Dragana," I shouted, "get out, please!" I was afraid for her. Her face looked gray with cold.

Her cousins were shouting for her to get out, too. "You'll get sick! It's too cold!"

She wouldn't listen. She wasn't going to give up on her brother.

Her cousins should be helping her, I thought. It wasn't enough to shout from the side of the river. They should get into the water and help her look. All these words weren't doing her any good.

I didn't think it was possible that Bojan could still be alive. The longer Dragana stayed in the river, the more I feared for her own safety. I felt weak and was wet with perspiration. All my energy went into holding myself upright but it was hard knowing that my friend was in that cold river and her little brother was at the bottom of it.

That was the first time I ever hated our river.

2

___

Azem & Tajib: My Brothers, My Heroes

Two of my younger brothers, Samir and Almir, were twins.
They would get up very early to spend their summer mornings
together fishing at the river. Later, they would sell what they
caught and come home with a present for my mother.

Samir loved to drink coffee even though he was only twelve.
My mother liked coffee, too, so Samir always bought her some
with his fishing money. He was so happy to be able to say to her,
"Mama, do you want coffee? I bought some and brewed it up for
us."

She would be doing some sort of work and she'd look up
to tell him, "Samir, don't spend your money on coffee! I have
coffee! Buy something for yourself."

"Almir and I made a lot of money. We have enough to share!"

It was not a lot of money, really, and Samir usually spent his
last coins the day that he earned them. But he was happy when
he could make someone else happy. He'd get my mother to cook

something nice that he could take to the cafés for the waiters. Samir was easy to like and most of his friends were people older than he.

His dream was to be a professional soccer player and when he wasn't fishing with Almir, he was at the stadium. But his dream might not have been terribly realistic—he was very weak and thin.

Almir, on the other hand, was strong and stocky. He didn't have many friends because when he wasn't fishing with Samir, he was swimming or diving alone. He practically lived in the river. Everyone knew him but they knew him as Samir's brother, the diver. The boys had the same face.

My father didn't know what a good high-diver Almir was until one day while on his way home from work, he saw many people crowded on the bridge and thought that there had been an accident. Instead, he was surprised to find that everyone was watching his son preparing to make another dive.

When he watched how beautifully Almir turned in the air and knifed into the water, my father was proud, but what he showed instead was anger. He was afraid for his son. When Almir came out of the river, my father made him go home. But my brother loved diving and nobody could stop him. The next day, he was at it again.

Almir's dream was to go to Mostar and dive from the bridge there. The Mostar bridge was old and famous, standing like a green rainbow over the river, Neretva. People came from all over the world every year to watch the diving competition from the bridge.

"When I dive in Mostar," Almir would tell my mother, "you'll be very proud of me."

"I'd be happier if you didn't dive at all," she'd tell him. But all of her children were in some way drawn to the rivers.

That October day when little Bojan drowned in the cold waters of the Drina, no one could persuade Dragana to come ashore and get warm. People on the bridge and along the shore looked on, horrified or worried, but no one helped Dragana search and no one brought her out of the river.

There were tears on my mother's cheeks. I heard her catch her breath as she saw some movement below the bridge.

It was my brothers Azem and Tajib and their friend, Ibrahim. Ibrahim was tying a rope around Azem's waist. Dragana saw them, too, and she was finally willing to be coaxed out of the water. Her cousins helped her ashore.

Ibrahim was like another brother to me. His father, Salko, used to call both Azem and Tajib his sons. Ibrahim's father fretted over the knot they were tying.

"Don't worry, Salko," Azem assured him. "It's good and tight. I'll be careful." To Ibrahim he said, "I'm ready."

"Give the rope a light pull every now and then to let us know you're okay," said Ibrahim. "If you don't feel good, yank it hard and we'll pull you in."

"If you get very cold," Tajib said, "get out and let me go. Don't stay in too long."

"I'm very cold already," Azem joked. They wished him luck.

All this time, my mother said nothing. She watched them and I knew she was afraid for her son but she wouldn't show it. She dried her tears and though she said nothing, I am sure that she put her faith in God. Azem was a good swimmer and surely God would help someone who was helping others.

I felt stronger, watching my mother.

People were calling out to Azem, wishing him luck and telling him where to look. Then he disappeared under the surface. With that, everyone grew silent. For the long, long time that he was under the water, no one said a word.

He seemed to be down forever. Was he all right? I looked at the rope to see if I could tell when he was pulling it. It did seem to move a little in Tajib and Ibrahim's hands.

We watched the river.

His head bobbed out of the water and he gasped for air. When he could speak, he said, "I saw him. My God, he is there, he is there. I saw him, there on the bottom."

His face looked terrible. I had never seen such an expression on my brother's face before, never seen him dealing with something that was too much for him.

"I can't do it," he said. "I'm sorry, but I can't bring him." I think I understood. My brother, who was always volunteering, who helped out wherever help was needed, he had a heart big enough to help. But he didn't have the heart to bring little Bojan's body from the bottom. He wanted to remember Bojan as the little noisy boy who always had a smile. "Azem," called Tajib. His voice was full of worry. "Azem, get out of the river. I'll do it."

"Okay," answered Azem. "I'll show you where he is and you can get him."

Azem was shaking when he climbed from the cold water into the cold air. He stood, shivering, clutching his shoulders, nodding to the place where he had seen Bojan's body and describing the shape of the river bottom to Tajib. Then he untied the rope and helped Ibrahim tie it around Tajib's waist.

When Tajib dove under the water, there was silence again. Everyone watched the spot where Azem had surfaced. I looked at my mother. Now her face was red and she had turned away from the river. She knew her children, knew that Tajib would do as he said and she didn't want to see what the little boy looked like after all this time under the river.

When Tajib surfaced, people started talking.

My brother struggled to the shore, holding the little boy in the air. He held Bojan by his pants as he climbed out of the water. You could see Tajib's hope by the way he carried Bojan.

"Maybe he's not dead!" I heard people around me say. "Children can be under the water for a long time and live," I heard someone else say.

Tajib shouted for someone to call the hospital, but someone else looked at the little boy's body and said, "No, I'm sorry. He is dead."

No one wanted to believe that our Drina had taken this child from us. But others looked and agreed. Bojan was dead.

The voice of Bojan's mother rose above all the others. "Bojan, my son, your mother bought books for you so that you could go to school."

People stopped talking. No one knew where to look. She screamed and cried out, "Bojan, my son, your mother cannot live without you!" Her voice cut my heart.

"Bojan, my son, I made clothes for you. How can your mother look at your clothes for all her life?"

I never knew why the Serbs always did this when somebody died. They repeated everything that had happened in that person's life. Bojan's mother didn't cry but she went on repeating the events of his short life.

Bojan's father was not at the river. He came to our apartment later and told my mother that she was a fortunate woman to have children who were so good to other people.

"I'll never forget what Azem and Tajib did for me," he said. "You know, Naza, it would have been harder if we weren't able to put Bojan to rest in the cemetery. If not for your sons, he would have stayed in the Drina forever."

"No, Burdus," my mother said. "If my boys hadn't brought him out, someone else would have done it."

"You have brought your children up well. I don't know what I can say, how I can tell you..."

"It's all right, Burdus. It's okay. When a little time has passed, we will talk. You should be with your family. There was no need to come say thank you. We're all here to help each other."

"Where are they? Where are Azem and Tajib?"

My mother never lied. She did then. "They're at Ibrahim's house. You can go home and I'll tell them you were here." When he had gone, my mother went to check on my brothers. They were both in bed with high fevers and chills—they were sick for days. And for months after that, they had terrible nightmares.

Bojan's father never knew.

3

The River Runs Sweet

Summer 1988

Even in summer, the Drina wasn't really pleasant for swimming but since our annual swimming competitions were in that river, it was the one to practice in. Otherwise, I preferred the Rzav.

Getting to the beach on the banks of the Rzav in the summer afternoons was a contest in itself. That part of the river was a long walk for most of us since young people didn't own cars.

If you hitchhiked successfully, you could get to the beach ahead of everyone else and claim a good spot. If not, you settled for what was left. The lucky ones who got rides always teased the ones who didn't. If you were lucky, it was cause for celebration for the rest of the day. If you didn't get a ride, you were quiet.

One particular day, my younger sister had been lucky. I had watched her leave the house with her friends, riding with one girl's father. As I got ready to leave the house myself, I imagined that Amira was at that very moment teasing some of her friends at the beach. The ride in the car would mean that my sister and her companions had a place to sit and the new arrivals did not. "Well of course there isn't a place for you," Amira would be saying. "What do you expect when you're such slowpokes?"

My sister's voice, like mine, was loud. That was one of the ways we were alike. Her hair was long and brown, a little bit darker than mine. Like mine, her eyes were brown. And even though she was just thirteen, she went to the cafés with her friends and slept at each other's houses once a week—the kinds of things that girls my age did. She and her friends had serious conversations for hours, too, like you'd expect of someone older. She loved dancing with her friends at the disco or going camping with them. Whenever you'd see Amira, you'd see her eight best friends around her.

Amira would always tell you exactly what she thought, even if it hurt your feelings. I wasn't like that, but otherwise we were practically the same.

On that day, even though I wasn't heading for the Rzav, I had been lucky, too. My older brother, Tajib, was in Sarajevo, which meant that I could borrow his motorcycle without having to ask. My friend, Sabina, had her own motorcycle and we rode together to the Drina.

It was late July and very warm. The sun was bright and the people we met at the river smiled and greeted one another happily.

My friend, Vahid, was already getting ready to swim. I asked Sabina if she'd mind my swimming with him to practice since Vahid and I were both preparing for the August competition.

I had started swimming for my city's swimming team when I was twelve and we swam against the teams from cities all around us. In July, there was always the regional mini-Olympics which spanned five days of competitions. It was held in a different city each year and athletes representing about fifty cities from Serbia, Montenegro and Bosnia took part. But the competition that really counted for day-to-day bragging rights was the August swim, the local contest to see who was the best swimmer in Visegrad. "Go ahead and practice with him," Sabina said. "I won't get lonely." She had been born in that area of Visegrad, Dusce, there by the Drina, and she knew every other person we saw. "Are you ready to really swim hard?" Vahid asked me with a smile. He was a very good swimmer, much better than I was, and once he started swimming he would keep going and going and going.

"Let me keep up with you," I reminded him.

"Just swim fast and there won't be any problem," he told me.

Then we were swimming. Vahid cut the water with long, powerful strokes. He was holding back but I still had to swim my hardest to keep up with him. When we were almost across, I had to stop for a moment to tread water. Vahid looked back at me and stopped.

My heart was pounding. I was short of breath and my arms felt weak. I wasn't used to sprinting like that. "Can we rest?" I asked him. "I'm very tired."

"We can rest at the wall," he said. "We're almost there, Jasmina. Just a little farther." The current swept us along. We both started swimming again.

I made it to the wall. It was concrete with holes under the water where you could stand for a while and rest. As the current swept me along the face of the wall, I felt for the holes. By then I was exhausted. I could hardly stay afloat and the wall was smooth everywhere I felt. "Vahid!" I cried. "I can't find them! Where are the holes!"

It wasn't Vahid who answered. From close by, a very calm voice said, "Jasmina, this way. You can find a place to stand over here." A boy I didn't know had appeared next to me in the water.

As the stranger guided me to a resting place in the wall, I felt several things at once. First, I was relieved to be able to rest. But I was also a little peeved. How did this boy know my name? Clearly, he knew Vahid, too, as he assured my friend that I was all right.

As he stood in another hole in the wall, I looked at him and started to feel something else.

He had amazing blue eyes—I could see the whole world in them. His brown hair was long, almost to his shoulders. That was unusual among Bosnian boys but very becoming on him. A few wet strands clung to his cheeks and river water streamed from his mane onto his shoulders.

We talked. That is, Vahid and this boy talked while I held onto the wall looking at him. After a while, Vahid swam off somewhere and I had to think of things to say.

I didn't mean to stare and I tried not to be obvious. I was surprised to find myself so interested. With my friends in school, I had joked about how this boy or that boy looked. But I had never looked at a boy and felt what I was feeling now as I clung wetly to a concrete wall.

Vahid's voice woke me from my dream. "Jasmina, do you want to go back?" He had found a big inner tube. "I can float with you to the other side and come back myself."

What I wished I could say was that Vahid should swim to the other side and leave me here with his friend. But the only thing I dared to say was, "Yes. Of course. Sabina is waiting for me. We have to go home soon."

In fact, if I didn't get home right away, my brother might arrive in time to see that I had taken his motorcycle. He would be furious.

All I could do was ask Vahid a few questions as he ferried me back across the Drina. "You know, Vahid, you never told me that you have such a nice friend."

"Who, Suljo?"

"Does he have a girlfriend?"

Vahid laughed. "Why do you want to know?"

I must have blushed. Vahid laughed again but he didn't tease me any more. "No, he doesn't have a girlfriend. One girl from your neighborhood liked him. You know, Tanja. But he didn't like her."

I knew Tanja very well. She lived in the building across from mine. Now I remembered. She had told us all about this boy. Suljo Ramic. Lots of girls liked him, she said, but he didn't care. If he didn't like Tanja or those other girls, what were the chances that he would like me?

"Jasmina," said Vahid, "I'll tell him that you like him."

"Are you crazy?"

"Suljo's my friend. I can tell him something like that. Maybe he'll like you, too."

"Vahid, don't! Please don't! I would die!"

"Okay, okay," he said. "I didn't know you were so shy." On the other side of the river, after Vahid was out of hearing, I told Sabina that I had met a very nice boy. "He's gorgeous," I told her. "I don't think I can describe how good looking he is. Do you know him? His name is Suljo."

"Suljo? Of course I know him. He's my cousin."

I refused to believe her at first. Her cousin? Visegrad was a small city and the people who lived there had grown up together. Everybody knew everybody else's family and talked about them, too. How had I missed this boy? For the first time, the thought crossed my mind that this was a little gift from God. I hadn't met Suljo until the moment was right.

"We can go to his house for coffee right now," Sabina said. We got on the motorcycles and she led the way.

4

In Search of Suljo

Suljo lived in Dusce, a neighborhood that was separated from the rest of Visegrad by a kilometer of empty road.

I don't know why there was a rivalry between Dusce and the rest of the city. It wasn't as if it were the poor part of town. In all of Visegrad, expensive houses commonly stood next to simple ones. But Dusce was often the butt of jokes. If you were talking about someone behind her back, a good put-down would always be, "Well, what can you expect? She's from Dusce." Then you'd laugh and make more jokes. One result of this attitude was that the people from Dusce always stuck together. If you bothered one of them, the rest would come after you. They were always together at school, always waited to walk home together. If you saw them in the cafés, it was a group of twenty together. Maybe it was that very separateness and solidarity that made people resent Dusce.

As Sabina and I drove the motorcycles up to Suljo's house, Sabina said, "There's his sister."

I knew the girl. We had gone to elementary school together. She had blue eyes, like Suljo's, and long blond hair. Unfortunately, my friends and I had never liked her because she was from Dusce.

We parked the motorcycles and went into the yard. Suljo's sister didn't seem very happy to see me there. I couldn't blame her. My friends and I had been rotten to her. My head filled with excuses. It wasn't my fault that all of Visegrad felt that way about her neighborhood.

"Maybe we should go home," I told Sabina.

"Okay," Sabina said. "I'm just going to say hello to my family. You stay here with Suljo's sister for ten minutes and then we'll go."

Then Sabina was gone and I was standing with Suljo's sister. When I had finally met a boy I liked so much, why did his sister have to be the one person in the world who must hate me? I tried to think of something to say. Instead, she broke the silence.

"How do you like the beach here?"

The banks of the Drina didn't compare to the Rzav, and in any case, it certainly wasn't a beach. Just grass that bordered the river. I said, "It's nice, but you know, I don't know many people here."

Then I had to try to think of something else to say. The longer Sabina was inside the house, the angrier I was. I couldn't believe that she was leaving me out here alone. Suljo's sister didn't seem to be trying very hard to think of something else to say. For an eternity of ten minutes, neither of us spoke.

Finally, Sabina reappeared and we rode home.

I was happy and sad at the same time. It was a relief to get out of Dusce but I was disappointed that Suljo hadn't come home while I was there. Very soon, I had something different to think about as I saw my brother waiting for me. He had come home first.

Tajib looked for a moment as if he couldn't decide between anger and surprise. To keep me from using the motorcycle, he had drained the gas from the tank. What he hadn't thought about was that when you're fifteen years old, there's always a way.

"Jasmina," he said, "when I tell you not to do something, that means that you don't do it!"

Because fathers in Bosnia were away at work during the day and were at home during the evening when younger people were at the cafés, a girl's older brothers had as much authority over her as her parents did. It was my brother's responsibility to look after me. When I wanted to go somewhere, if I wanted to have a boyfriend, if I wanted to stay out late, I had to get my brother's permission. Being in trouble with Tajib was as bad as being in trouble with my father.

I stood next to the motorcycle and let him chew me out. I knew he wouldn't go on yelling for very long because it was five p.m., the beginning of our family rush hour.

There were two bathrooms in our apartment and nine children. During the summer, this was the time of day when everyone wanted to shower and grab something to eat. We had to hurry, because by five-thirty all the young people of Visegrad would be at the Sports Center. As soon as I'd get my turn in the shower, someone would knock on the door and tell me to hurry up. It drove me crazy.

After fifteen minutes of frenzy, we'd all be out the door again. My poor mother. All summer, we hardly came home except to shower and grab a bite to eat. She'd barely get to say hello to us before we were gone and she was alone with my father.

Tajib looked at his watch, frowned, and told me I'd better

never touch his motorcycle again without asking. I hurried inside
to get ready to go.

5

A Crush & Ice Cream on a Summer Night

The Sports Center in Visegrad was great. It was the most famous place in the city and not only for athletes and spectators. To get to the Center, you had to cross a bridge over the confluence of the Rzav and the Drina. The point of land where the rivers met was called Usce and there was a restaurant there by that name. Next to the Usce was a square screened all around by weeping willows—a good place for lovers to meet. There were more willows along the river with benches beneath them. Footpaths led from the river up to the Usce and down on the other side to the Sports Center. During the day, people came to that part of town to sing, play music and talk. With water on either side, the area near the Center was like an island. It was one of those magical places where you felt that the rest of the world was far, far away.

This faraway little world was only fifty meters from my home. It was part of the reason that I was sure I could never live anywhere but Visegrad. We had the Sports Center, the rivers and all the little cafés where you could always find someone you knew. The only thing I didn't love about Visegrad was that you couldn't have any secrets there. In my little city, nothing travelled faster than news.

When I arrived at the Sports Center, everyone there seemed to know about Suljo. We started to play volleyball and between serves all my friends asked me questions about what had happened at the river. I acted as if I were concentrating on my game instead of the questions but really I was thinking about Suljo. What should I wear later when we all went out to the cafés? I might see Suljo there and I'd want to impress him. I tried to remember all the clothes I owned but nothing seemed quite right.

What was happening to me? Suljo was only a boy, right? It wasn't such a big deal. But it was. Suljo wasn't like any other boy I had met. I was glad that he wasn't there at the Center. I felt shy enough as it was.

When the volleyball game was over, I couldn't have told you the score. I don't think I even noticed who won.

Back home later, I had given up on my own wardrobe and was looking through my sister's clothes when I heard my friends arriving and greeting my mother. "Mukadesa," I asked my sister, "can I wear this shirt?" As soon as she said I could, I wasn't sure it was what I wanted after all.

Senada and Dragana came in. "Is that what you're wearing?" Senada said. "It's nice."

"Hey, Mukadesa, can I borrow your black shirt?" Dragana asked. She was a little bit fat and always asked for black clothes to make her look thinner.

In our family, among our friends and generally in our city, people shared. My older brothers, Tajib and Azem, and my older sister, Mukadesa, gave me money if I asked for it. And whenever I had money, I bought drinks—sodas, juices and coffee—for my friends while it lasted. When my money ran out, my friends bought drinks for me. It was the same for clothes. Every evening as people headed to the cafés, you could see them on the street taking off their shirts or shoes and handing them to each other. Everyone shared everything and it was a funny sight to see people negotiating wardrobe exchanges and changing clothes as they walked down the street.

My sister, Mukadesa, served as a boutique. She had beautiful clothes so everybody came to ask her for something to wear and then went home to dress.

"I don't have much money for tonight," Senada was telling me. "I gave most of it to Ramo."

That was good news, actually.

Ramo was her older brother. Senada was always giving him money. He played soccer and also worked a regular job but whatever he earned was spent long before he had it. He'd tell the waiter to bring a round of drinks for everyone at his table, promising to pay, "When the team pays me or when I get my salary."

In Visegrad, you could always pay later. The waiters all knew you and trusted that you'd be back again to settle the tab once you had the money. But you couldn't count on such liberal credit in another city.

If Ramo had cash to spend, he and Tajib would usually dress up and go to another city together. Senada never asked her brother where he was going, but she asked Tajib.

"Why are you asking me?" Tajib said. "Why aren't you asking Ramo?" But he was dressed up. Almost certainly, they were going out of town. Great! With Tajib and Ramo away, we could stay in the cafés longer.

Senada adored her brother and would have given him the money in any case but we didn't mind that there was a side benefit to supplying Ramo with spending money.

Later, after Senada and Dragana had gone home to get ready, Selma, Dijana and Sabina arrived. The three of them were my best friends, the ones I hung out with every day.

Selma's family was rich—not that you'd know that by looking at her or talking to her. She had an apartment in Sarajevo that her parents bought for her when she started to attend the university there. Many of us took trips to Sarajevo to buy clothes—what you could find in Visegrad wasn't as fashionable—and we'd all sleep at Selma's apartment. Since Sarajevo hotels were expensive, sometimes there would be twenty of us from Visegrad on a clothes expedition, sleeping at Selma's.

Dijana's family was strict and she was an only child. She couldn't always do the things Selma, Sabina and I wanted to do because her parents were so protective. We all hated the ritual of persuading her parents to let her do something fun. They would ask, "Where are you going? Who are you going with? Who else will be there? Jasmina, is this all right with your parents? How are you going to get there? What will you do?"

After grilling us all for about an hour, they would give her permission to go out for an hour and a half. Whenever we were really beginning to have a good time someplace, Dijana would have to go home.

Sabina's family were shopkeepers and the store they owned was like a café for the four of us. We would meet there and talk for hours. Sometimes the store was even better than a café because we could talk about all kinds of things without being overheard. Sabina always knew the best gossip. It was, I guess, part of her family's trade. In Visegrad, the stores were like headquarters for information. After all, everybody had to buy groceries, and a lot of people would tell the shopkeepers what was going on in their own lives so the shopkeepers knew everything. Of course, being friends with a great information source like Sabina cut both ways. As my mother called through the bathroom door, "Jasmina! Your friends are here," I was sure that Sabina had already told Selma and Dijana about Suljo.

I prayed that my mother wouldn't tell them how long I had been in the bathroom primping.

"I'm coming! I'll be out in a minute!"

When I came out, my friends were all smiling. "You look good," Selma said.

"Especially good," said Sabina. "Did it take you long to get so gussied up?"

I shrugged. "Ten minutes," I said. "Shall we go?"

"Ten minutes!" my mother said. "You've been in that bathroom for at least half an hour. At least! I couldn't get in there myself because you were using it so long. If this were your wedding day, you would have been faster!"

My mother had no idea how much teasing I was going to be in for now. She made me blush, too, at the mention of marriage. True, I had just met Suljo, but the thought had already crossed my mind.

"Well," said Dijana, "we can tell you took a lot of time. You look great."

"Yes," said Selma. "But why make such an effort for tonight? Is tonight special?"

My mother, thank heaven, did not catch on. As far as she was concerned, I always spent far too much time getting ready to go out with my friends.

"Let's stop standing around," I said.

Outside of the apartment, I told them, "Well, if you must

know why I made a special effort to look nice, it's like this: If you want to catch a good looking boy, you'd better look good yourself."

"Aha!" said Selma. "So that's it!"

"As if you didn't already know," I said, looking at Sabina.

"Well, of course I had to tell them," Sabina said. "We're your friends. It's our right to know which boy you like."

"Do you really think I look all right?"

"Jasmina," said Selma, "You look smashing."

I hoped Suljo would think so. I was wearing a close-cut long black dress and a brown jacket about the color of my hair. My hair was very short and I had gelled it back. I wore silver earrings. In spite of all the effort I had put in, my heart felt weak. I knew my legs would be shaking as soon as I saw Suljo.

"We know him," Selma said.

"I had a crush on him in elementary school."

"Really?"

"Alma, Jasna and I used to watch when he played soccer in front of the school. He's very nice, really. We all know him. I thought for sure you already knew him because he and Vahid are best friends."

"I can't believe this. I just saw him for the first time in my life."

"Where have you been all this time? Are you sure you live in Visegrad?"

It really was strange not to have seen a good-looking boy who had grown up in Visegrad but it wasn't totally unbelievable. There were two big elementary schools side by side and your family chose which one they wanted to send you to. Selma, Sabina, Dijana, Vahid and Suljo had all gone to one. Senada, Dragana, my brothers, sisters and I had gone to the other.

"He plays soccer with Tajib and Azem," said Dijana. "We're pretty sure Mukadesa knows him, too."

It was reassuring to hear that my brothers knew and apparently liked Suljo, but it also felt strange that everyone around me knew him while he'd been invisible to me. Again, I thought that perhaps he was a gift from God. I felt more sure of myself. Maybe Suljo was meant to fall in love with me, just as I had been instantly attracted to him.

When we arrived on Capital Street, it was crowded with people. From five p.m. on, the street was closed to cars but there was a traffic jam of pedestrians since everyone came out to stroll before going to the cafés. There were three cafés on Capital Street and in summer they put tables outside, almost in the street itself.

I don't know how many people I bumped into that night as I craned my neck to see over shoulders, failing to see where I was going. I was looking for Suljo. I knew where Vahid and his friends usually sat—on the steps of the Municipal Building—but when we got there I saw only my sister, Mukadesa, and many of our friends. There were maybe a dozen of them sitting on the steps. Someone was strumming a guitar and they were chatting and watching people stroll by.

"Hey," said my sister, "what's up with the four of you?"

"Nothing much," said Selma.

"Don't lie," said Eta, the girl sitting next to Mukadesa. "Where is Suljo? Our Jasmina has fallen in love."

I felt my face get hot. Everyone knew! Several people in the group grinned at me.

"Jasmina, can you go buy ice cream for all of us?" Mukadesa asked.

Rescued by my sister! I was relieved to escape from the teasing that was sure to get worse. "Sure," I said. "Why not?"

Every night that we hung out on those steps, somebody went to buy ice cream for the whole crowd. The ice cream stand was only a few meters from the steps, just around a wall. As I turned the corner, I realized that my sister hadn't been coming to my rescue after all.

Suljo and Vahid were sitting on the wall, right next to the ice cream stand. When I saw them, my knees went wobbly. I felt as if I were about to fall flat on my face.

I froze. I couldn't take a step forward but I certainly couldn't retreat back to where Mukadesa and the others were sitting. Should I just keep walking up the street?

I turned around. My friends were laughing.

Ice cream, I thought. *I am just here for ice cream.*

I had just stepped closer to the ice cream vendor, bringing me within an arm's length of the wall when I heard Suljo's voice from above, "Hey, Jasmina! Don't you want to say 'hi' to us?"

I looked up. My knees were shaking and I desperately hoped it wasn't obvious.

"Oh. Hi." I said. "How are you? I didn't see you guys up there. I was thinking about something else."

I sounded like a little girl trying to talk her way out of trouble for something she knew she had done. I could feel the heat in my face, I must have been bright red. I wanted to take another step toward the ice cream stand but my gaze was fixed on Suljo. He had an easy smile and he looked incredible, dressed in white with a light blue sweatshirt tied around his shoulders. The shirt and his eyes were the same color. It was getting hard to breathe.

"So what's up?" said Vahid.

"I'm buying ice cream for my friends."

"I hope you'll share some with us," said Suljo.

"Of course she will," said Vahid, "But she should give me

more than you. Jasmina is my friend and she hardly knows you, Suljo. Isn't that right, Jasmina?"

I could have killed Vahid. Instead I said, "Um, I'll see. I have to go!"

I had never before understood older people when they talked about love, about getting tongue-tied, about being unable to concentrate. Now, looking at Suljo, I understood it all.

I hurried to buy the ice cream. I expected to turn and at least say goodbye to Suljo but when I looked at the wall again, he and Vahid were gone. It was as if I had dreamt them.

When I returned to the steps, though, there they were, sitting with everyone else. When I arrived with the ice cream, Suljo was smiling again, very gently. I smiled back. I think that we communicated something with our smiles but I didn't dare speak to him, not in front of all my friends. He seemed shy, too, and didn't talk to me. But he did talk to everyone else. I could see that he and Mukadesa seemed to be old friends. I felt a little strange—he talked to them so casually but I had a hard time talking to him.

So while Suljo talked with everybody else, Vahid and I chatted off to the side.

"He likes you," Vahid said quietly.

"You told him?" I was delighted and mortified.

"He thinks you are nice but you are still very young and a little bit thin. When you get older, he is sure you will be a very beautiful woman. But he has one problem. He is very good friends with your brothers, Azem and Tajib. He doesn't think it would be right to be with you because of your brothers."

"That's stupid! In Visegrad everyone is friends with everyone else. No, that can't be a problem."

Perhaps it wasn't quite true that everyone was everyone else's friend, but it was true that Azem and Tajib were friends with everybody. If that were an obstacle to romance, I would never have a boyfriend.

"Don't be angry with me," Vahid said. "I'm just telling you what Suljo told me. It won't be a problem. I know that. The two of you will be together."

"I hope so."

"You know, Jasmina, you should get me together with one of your friends."

Aha! Vahid had liked one of my friends all this time but had been too shy to tell me. He could tell me now, because I had told him about Suljo.

"Okay. Tell me which one you like?"

"I like your friend Alma."

"Alma," I said, looking toward the rest of the group. "Okay, I'll tell her."

"But not right now! When you're alone with her you can talk to her about me. At swimming practice, you can tell me what she said."

Alma was my cousin and my friend. She had long black hair and black eyes. She was a very nice girl but she wasn't like the rest of us. We were born the same year and grew up on the same street in adjacent buildings but she didn't play sports and she hardly ever went out with the rest of us. She stayed home and watched TV. In fact, I was a little surprised to see her there on the steps with the rest of us.

"Vahid, I'll talk to her. Be thankful that you're getting to see her tonight. She doesn't go out, you know."

"I know. It doesn't matter."

While Vahid and I were talking, Suljo interrupted us. "What are you two talking about?"

"About politics," said Vahid.

Selma laughed. "That's Jasmina for you. All the way over

here, all she wanted to do was talk about politics. It's the only thing on her mind."

Suljo reminded Vahid that they had practice in the morning. "We should go," he said.

I was disappointed. I had hardly spoken to Suljo and now he was going home.

"Okay, you're right," said Vahid, but then he said, "Where are you going now, Nova Mahala?"

Nova Mahala was the name of our neighborhood. "We're going to our steps," someone said. "They're the best steps in Visegrad."

Hanging out on the steps was something of a tradition for young people. All over the city, you'd see people clustered on steps to chat, joke around, play the guitar and sing. The steps of Nova Mahala were very special to my friends and me. They were under a store at an intersection of Capital Street and another, smaller street. Two cafés were nearby.

We all gathered on those steps every night of the summer. We'd be there by eleven o'clock or midnight after we had come home from the cafés and changed clothes again back into something more casual. For me and my friends, it was the best part of the day, the most relaxed time. None of my friends brought their girlfriends or boyfriends to the steps because we felt it was a place only for the people from Nova Mahala.

Sometimes the older women in our neighborhood would make a cake for us. These were the same women who were often mad at us because we stayed so late on the steps and made so much noise, keeping them from sleep. They would appear in their windows and call down, "Tomorrow we'll tell your mothers and fathers how noisy you were!"

Then we would be quiet for a few minutes while they fell

asleep. Often we were on those steps until three or four in the morning.

The next day, there would be a price to pay. At Sabina's store, those old women would tell everyone who was noisiest. And we all dreaded being sent to the store in the morning for bread.

"You, Dervisevic!" the women would say. "You, Nurko's daughter! You were very loud last night!"

They would call us by our last names or our fathers' names. They didn't know our first names, just our faces and which family we belonged to.

"It's not true!" I would say. "I wasn't even there last night!" It did no good to lie. Everyone knew all about you. In my neighborhood, everyone knew what you'd had for dinner at home. But how could you fail to defend yourself? All the shoppers in the store would be staring at you. And word would soon get back to your parents, you could count on that. Sometimes it seemed as if there were a competition among the people in the store—who would be the first at your apartment to tell your family about you. But they were often giving my mother information she already had. On mornings when my brothers, sisters and I fought about who had to go to the store, she knew.

When you'd been singled out as one of the noisiest, you'd be "in jail" for a few nights. That's what we called being grounded. After a jail term, when we reappeared on the steps with our friends, the women would bring cake they had made to cheer us up and soften any hard feelings.

That night after the ice cream incident, I was voluntarily "in jail." I was too sad to go sit on the steps. I hadn't really talked to Suljo at all.

6

Visegrad Heaven

By the time school started again in September, Suljo was my boyfriend. We spent as much time as we could together though our school schedules made it difficult since we were on different tracks.

Suljo was in his third year of high school—the same as being a junior in an American high school, except that Suljo's third year would be his last. In Bosnia, only the students who planned for careers in professions like medicine, engineering, or management continued through a fourth year. Most students were destined for jobs as waiters, carpenters or mechanics, so they graduated at the end of their third year.

I was in my second year with plans to stay through all four years of school. I wanted to be a furniture designer and my test scores after the first year of high school had been high enough to support my ambition.

As luck would have it, third year students like Suljo had

classes from one in the afternoon to six in the evening. My second-year classes started at eight in the morning and got out just before his began which somewhat complicated our romance. Suljo's solution was to meet me every day as soon as my last class was over. After walking me home, he sprinted back to school, routinely arriving at his first class late and out of breath.

Jasmina & Suljo walking on the path around the Visegrad
Sports Center along The Drina River

That first class was Serbo-Croatian, which would be like an

English class in the U.S. Each week, the teacher assigned a topic for an essay. One week, Suljo's assignment was, "To write about something or someone very important to you." After walking me home and dashing back to school one day, Suljo opened the door of the classroom to hear the professor reading aloud Suljo's essay about our love. Suljo was so embarrassed. He was still breathing hard and everyone in the class knew why he was late and where he had been. As Suljo crossed the room to his seat, wishing he could turn invisible, the students practically fell out of their chairs laughing at him.

By now, almost everyone knew about Suljo and me. One of my teachers, Pero Mitrovic, lived on my street right around the corner from my family's apartment. He was a Serb who taught physical education. Suljo always met me in front of his building and would say goodbye to me there, too. We would hug and kiss and then I'd run home. We never dared to do that in front of my family's apartment—my father would have killed me.

One day in class, Pero called out to me, "Jasmina!"

I didn't know what he wanted but I supposed I was in trouble again. I always talked to my friends in that class and Pero was constantly scolding me for it. He said that I drove him crazy because I was his best athlete but for the whole year he had to mark me down from a grade of five to two for talking. (At the end of the year, he relented and gave me a five. I was his best student after all.)

"Jasmina," he said again so that he had the attention of the whole class, "I want to thank you."

I was relieved at not being in trouble, but confused.

"Thank me?"

"Yes, Jasmina, for taking such good care of my car. Nobody will steal the tires with you and Suljo sitting on it all the time!"

The whole class burst out laughing but I wasn't embarrassed like Suljo had been. I laughed right along with them.

Each grade in our school was divided into smaller groups depending on the course of study with each group having its own homeroom teacher. The homeroom teacher met with parents, discussed career plans with the students and keep up with their progress. If you wanted to leave school early for some reason or get permission to miss a day of classes, you needed clearance from your homeroom teacher.

The homeroom teacher for my group was Risto Perisic and he was often more like a kindly conspiratorial uncle than an authority figure. If I hadn't done my homework for some class, he would help me come up with an excuse. He would gladly grant just about any legitimate request from the students, though I don't mean to suggest that he didn't take his role seriously. That's why I was so surprised at what he offered one morning.

Suljo and I were waiting outside for my first class to begin. The classroom was locked which was fine with us—it gave us a few extra minutes to be together. Risto walked by and smiled as he saw us. Then he stopped and turned.

"Jasmina," he said, "do you want to take the day off and be with Suljo?"

"Of course!"

Risto raised his hand. "One day. Just today!" And he smiled again.

Weeks passed into months and soon Suljo and I had been seeing each other for almost a year. I know it sounds syrupy, but I was in heaven. Life in Visegrad had always been happy for me and now it was perfect. I thought things could never be better.

That's not to say I was perfectly delighted with every little thing that happened. For one thing, I was disappointed that Suljo and I could not go to his class graduation party together.

It was held in the Hotel Bikavac which looked down on the city from a hill in a stylish neighborhood. Boys got to choose their dates from students in any course of study but the date had to be someone from the graduating class.

A Bosnian graduation party was a little like a Senior Prom, including a real promenade. All the couples dressed to the nines and walked up and down the main street of Visegrad a few times to see and be seen. Lots of people gathered to see them and offer best wishes then talked for days about what this student or that one had worn. The whole month before the party, students hardly talked about anything other than what they were going to wear. They knocked themselves out to look their best.

I didn't feel totally left out. Suljo chose to go to the party with my friend, Djejna, so a bunch of us showed up at her house to help her with all the small details. She wore a tight black dress with a green jacket. My sister, Mukadesa, had done Djejna's hair and it looked spectacular.

When Suljo arrived in his suit, it was almost as if I were seeing him for the first time again. He always dressed well but tonight he was gorgeous.

"What do you think?" he said.

"I think you and Djejna are going to be the best looking couple tonight!"

I couldn't have been more proud to be his girlfriend. At the same time, I felt that little stab of regret again over not being able to go with him. Actually, what made me more sad was the thought of the time ahead. Suljo had plans to go to France for three months to visit an uncle who lived there.

Not long after the graduation party, when the time finally came for Suljo to leave for France, we spent the whole day before he left holding each other and crying. Suljo took one of my shirts with him so he could sleep with it every night and have my aroma near him. I took one of his sweaters to remind me of him every day, not that I would need reminding.

"I'm going to miss you like crazy, Jasmina!"

"Just hurry home!" I told him.

7

The Competition

Summer 1989

My first days without Suljo were very hard. When my mother gave me some money to buy shoes, I spent it on phone calls to him instead.

But June was a busy time and there were things to keep me occupied. Most important was the big July mini-Olympics competition. That year it was in Arilje, a small city in Serbia. For once, Visegrad was going to field only a small team of about thirty. Every year before, there had been more like a hundred and fifty of us. Still, this year's competitors from Visegrad were very good. With Suljo away, I probably practiced harder than I might have if he were around.

Arilje was the first place where I had a sense that things were changing in my country. In Arilje, they didn't fly the flag of Yugoslavia as they had the year before. Instead, they flew the Serbian flag of a hundred years ago. From some of the cafés, my friends and I could hear the songs that Chetniks had sung in World War II. It scared us.

I should say, it scared some of us.

Before this time, I hadn't given much thought to our differences. Although some of us were Muslims and some were Serbs, we all thought of ourselves as Yugoslavs. I know I didn't look at friends like Boba, Ceca or Dragana any differently because they were Serbs. The difference was just a matter of religion.

But now, in Arilje, there was a noticeable difference between us: the Serbs on our team didn't feel uncomfortable about this flag or these songs. They weren't threatened.

All of this had something to do with how I felt as I got ready to swim. The swim races were on the second day of the competition. I woke up nervous. On the relay team with Mukadesa, Bob and Ceca, I was the youngest and least powerful swimmer. To make matters worse, it was the second day of my menstruation. In our room, the frantic preparations of twenty women swimmers didn't help at all to settle me down. "Hey, 'Kadesa!" someone said to my sister. "Good luck in the relays!"

"Ceca! Boba! Good luck!" said someone else. "You, too, Jasmina!"

I'm going to need it, I thought.

We met the male swimmers in front of their room and then we all went together to the pool. When the ten of us arrived, there were already a lot of spectators. I started to shake. I wasn't the only one—who doesn't get nervous before a race? But it was worse for me than usual.

The women swam first. My sister, Mukadesa, won gold medals in the fifty, one hundred, and two hundred-meter races. Ceca took silver in the two hundred. Then it was time for the four of us to swim the relay race.

Boba was first off the starting block and she sped toward the far end of the pool. I was next, followed by Ceca and then Mukadesa, our anchor.

As I stepped onto the starting block, waiting for Boba to swim back and touch the wall, the swimmer next to me said something. She was from Titovo Uzice, a city in Serbia.

"Are you a good swimmer?" she asked again.

What a thing to ask, I thought. *And what a time to ask it.* "No. Not really," I said.

"Me neither," she said.

Boba, in first place, was nearing the wall, so that was the end of our conversation. Boba touched and I dove out over the water. Suddenly, I was swimming too hard to be nervous.

My leg of the relay went by in a blur. I made a clean turn, swam hard the whole way and when I touched the first wall again and Ceca dove in for the third leg, our coach lifted me out of the pool. Spectators were cheering on their favorites.

"Still in first!" he said. "We can't lose!" And he was right. Ceca and Mukadesa just extended our lead.

Six male swimmers from Visegrad took medals home as well. We felt as if we'd just swept the Olympics. Our coach went from swimmer to swimmer, kissing us and holding us up and sometimes waving his hands as if he was too happy to know what to do. Out of a total of thirty swimming medals, Visegrad won twenty-two!

Best of all was the medal ceremony before all the athletes and a huge crowd of spectators from Arilje. It really did feel like the Olympics. A feeling like that is one that stays with you forever. Is it any wonder that we were a little sports crazy in my family?

Little did we know, it was to be our last competition.

8

The Korana

The rest of the summer passed and on one August day, I was counting down the hours until Suljo's return. He had told me to expect him around ten that night. Every minute crawled by. When my parents wanted to go out and leave me in charge of my youngest brother, Emir, I was grateful for something to do.

At five, the doorbell rang. I went to the balcony and saw Djejna standing by our door.

"Hey, Djejna! What's up? Come upstairs."

"I can't come up. I have something for you. Can you come get it? I'm in a hurry."

"Okay. I'm coming."

Emir started to cry. "Please be a good boy," I told him. "I'll be back in a minute. I'm just going downstairs."

I ran down the stairs as quickly as I could. By then, Emir was really howling.

When I got to the bottom and looked around for Djejna, or

for whatever it was she left for me, someone grabbed me. Suljo lifted me into his arms and kissed me almost before I knew it was him.

I was so startled I didn't speak.

"Jasmina? Something wrong?"

"Nothing's wrong," I said. "You just surprised me."

But it was more than that. Suljo wasn't a boy any more. I could hardly believe how much he had changed in three months. He had cut his hair, but the real surprise was how much he had filled out, how much he had grown.

I forgot all about Emir until I heard him crying. I wanted to ask Djejna to look after him, but she had gone. Fortunately, Almir came home then and agreed to watch Emir so Suljo and I could go out.

"Jasmina," Suljo told me, "I made some money in France. I want to buy an engagement ring for you but I want you to pick out something you love. What do you think?"

"I think I love you more than anyone in this world!"

He bought me a beautiful ring that very evening. I was delighted to have him home and happier still to be engaged. Those next days together were glorious, but too few. While he was in France, Suljo's conscription notice had come, calling him into service with the Yugoslav Army. We had just fifteen days before he left again, this time for a year.

I was miserable but there wasn't anything we could do about it. Every young man Suljo's age had to serve. At the end of the fifteen days, Suljo's family had a huge going away party for him and there were similar parties going on all over the country. I spent most of the party crying which is the only reason I didn't cry the next day when we went to see him off at the bus stop. I had no tears left. I could see in Suljo's eyes that he didn't want to leave any more than I wanted to stay behind without him.

The send-off was another event that brought many people out onto the streets. Families and neighbors waited at the bus stop to say goodbye to the boys who were suddenly taking on the duties of young men.

I discovered that I had some tears left, after all. I bit them back. This was hard enough for Suljo without my falling to pieces. I told him, "Write me every day. I want to know what you're doing every day."

"I will," he said. "And you write me, too. Tell me all the news of Visegrad."

As his bus pulled away, I let the tears stream down my face. I cried the whole way home and I didn't care that people were looking at me. I went straight to my room and cried even harder. It already felt like Suljo had been gone for months.

A few days later, I came home from school and found his first letter. Seeing his handwriting on the envelope made me happy again.

"Jasmina," my mother said, "come have something to eat." She usually had something hot waiting for us after school—her cooking was so good that even some of our cousins would come to our house after school or work. "Look," she said, "I made something you love!"

"In a minute!" I ran to my room to savor every word Suljo had written to me.

His letter said that in a few days he would officially pledge his allegiance to the Yugoslav Army. He wanted me to come for the ceremony. The rest of the letter was him writing in a dozen different ways about how much he loved me.

After I read his letter, I had to disappoint my mother. I couldn't eat for the rest of the day. I started writing a letter back to him, telling him that I would be there for his allegiance day no matter what. Even if my parents wouldn't let me go, I wrote, I would find a way.

I meant what I wrote, though I wasn't sure how I'd get all the way to Karlovac, where he was serving. It was a town in Croatia, a sixteen-hour drive from Visegrad.

In the end, getting to Karlovac was easy. Suljo wrote to his parents that he didn't want to see them there without me so Suljo's father found my brother, Azem, in a café to ask permission for me to come. In fact, when Azem was a little reluctant, Suljo's father practically begged him. Azem relented but said my mother, father and oldest brother would also have to agree. My parents soon said it was all right for me to go. I even asked my homeroom teacher, Risto, for the day off from school and he granted it. But I still didn't have Tajib's permission.

I didn't handle the situation very diplomatically. I said to my oldest brother, "I'm going and that's all there is to it. Unless I die before the allegiance day, I'll be in Karlovac with Suljo."

"That's how you ask permission?" Tajib said. I had made him angry. "You're not going. You absolutely do not have my permission."

"Tajib, I will die if I can't go."

But Tajib just shook his head. I hadn't respected his authority as my brother.

The night before we were supposed to go, I couldn't sleep. I was going to see Suljo in spite of what Tajib said, since Tajib wouldn't be home when I left. Suljo would be so happy to see me—his parents hadn't been able to tell him for certain whether I was coming or not. I was already getting ready when the sun started to rise. Mukadesa got up early with me to do my hair and she gave me some money. My mother made breakfast but I couldn't eat.

"You'll be cold, Jasmina. Take a sweater."

I was more concerned with looking good than being warm. A sweater wouldn't go with what I was wearing but when my mother told me something like that, it was more than a suggestion. So I took a sweater. She, too, gave me some money, which surprised me. I had been saving money for the trip but I didn't work, so there wasn't much to save.

"Okay, mama. I'm leaving." I kissed her.

"Goodbye. And be careful!"

At Suljo's house in Dusce, his parents were waiting for me.

"Tell the truth," said Suljo's mother. "Did you escape or did your parents let you leave?" She wouldn't have let me go without my parents' permission.

"They let me go," I said. "My brother, Tajib, didn't say I could go but he wasn't there to stop me. He'll be mad but what can I do?" I reminded her that I had permission from my parents, Azem and my homeroom teacher, Risto.

The morning of the ceremony, it was cold and raining in Karlovac. The leaves had already turned and they fell from the trees with the rain. The early morning streets which ordinarily would have been almost empty were full of relatives arriving for the allegiance ceremony. Things were confusing. Army barracks were scattered throughout the city and all the people who didn't know the town were trying to find the right barracks in order to meet with their sons on time.

We got a little lost ourselves, so we were late. Many people had arrived ahead of us but it wasn't hard to spot Suljo waiting by the door. His parents were the first to make their way through the crowd and greet him. Then came his sister and brother-in-law. Suljo's uncle and I were behind them and I heard Suljo saying, "And Jasmina? Did you bring her? Did she come?"

"No," his mother teased. "She didn't want to come." Then he saw me and he smiled. He kissed his family first and I got used to seeing yet another change in him. His hair was even shorter and he was in a uniform that made him look bigger than he was.

People crowded and jostled all around us. They called out the names of their sons, searching, and twice someone stepped on my feet. I didn't care. I felt as if Suljo and I were the only ones there.

Finally he came and took me in his arms. I wanted to stay there forever, never leaving his embrace. We kissed and he didn't have to tell me how happy he was to see me. Too soon, he was saying, "I have to get ready. The ceremony starts soon." The ceremony was stirring, with all the excitement and precision of any formal military event. But the main thing I felt throughout was impatience. I wanted it to be over so I could have time with Suljo.

After the oaths had been sworn and the new soldiers broke ranks, Suljo came to tell us the good news. Three men from each unit had been granted a one-night leave so they could stay with their parents. Suljo was one of the lucky ones.

"There's a beautiful hotel called The Korana," he told us. "It's expensive but there's a great restaurant right there and nightclubs, too, so everyone says it's worth it."

"Then that's just what we want," said his father. So a short time later, we were sitting in the restaurant of The Korana, waiting for our lunch. Suljo's father registered for us and when he came back, Suljo's mother took one of the keys and leaned over to me.

"Jasmina, take the key to your and Suljo's room."

I was speechless and ecstatic. Suljo and I never dreamed that his parents would let us stay together in one room. Suljo also didn't know what to say but he was happy and grateful.

After lunch, Suljo's family went to their room to rest while Suljo and I took a walk around the city. Karlovac was beautiful.

In some ways, its parks, towering trees and river reminded me of Visegrad. Suljo showed me his favorite places—the riverside park close to the Hotel Korana where he read the letters I sent him and the apartment complex where the officers and their families lived.

"Do you like it? Isn't it a beautiful city?"

"It is, Suljo, but I don't know if it's just because I'm with you or if Karlovac really is beautiful."

Suljo took my hands in his. "They think I'd make a good officer, Jasmina. I'm being encouraged to try."

"You'd stay in the army?"

"We could live here permanently if I were an officer in the army."

"How could we do that? I have two more years of school still. I'd have to wait for you for an extra year. One year is bad enough!"

"Maybe you could finish school here in Karlovac. On an officer's pay, we'd live on a good salary and our apartment would be free."

We wanted to be married as soon as possible. In fact, we wanted to spend the rest of our lives together, starting at that very moment.

The future was still uncertain—Suljo wasn't an officer yet. But as I considered the possibility, I began to get used to the idea of living in Karlovac. We walked back to the hotel.

"This is a wonderful hotel," Suljo said, "don't you think? So elegant. We'll come back here for our honeymoon."

9

___

"This is Serbia."

Summer 1990

The next day brought another tearful farewell. We were getting lots of practice at it. That's how it is when you're young—you feel things strongly but you're not fully in charge of your life yet. You can't live out what you feel, can't go where you want to go or stay when you want to stay.

Still, I was happy about the time we'd had together. We'd been left alone together, truly and uninterruptedly alone, for the first time. I felt more closely bound to Suljo than ever.

Not even Tajib, who was waiting for me when I arrived back home, could take that away from me. He did intend to take everything else, though.

"You are in trouble like you've never been in trouble before," he said. "Do you want to go to the cafés tonight? Forget it. You're in jail. For the whole week. And the next time you want to go to Sarajevo for a shopping expedition, don't even bother to ask me. Who do you think you are? Do you ever think to listen when I tell you not to do something?"

I then did the worst thing I could do. I didn't mean to, but I looked at Tajib and I smiled. He reasonably assumed that I was making light of his authority, so he yelled some more and threatened me with worse punishments. But that was the very thing that had made me smile. There was nothing Tajib could do. I had my memories of Suljo safe in my heart.

On Monday morning, all my friends were waiting for me at the café in front of school. We met there every day.

"Well? Did you go?"

"I said I was going, didn't I?"

"Was Suljo happy to see you?"

"Think of a better question," I said.

"Tell us everything!"

But I just smiled.

"Well, you've got to buy all of us drinks, Jasmina. It's clear you had a good time. Fortune smiled on you."

It was a tradition. Good fortune obligated you to treat your friends to drinks in the café.

I decided not to tell anyone about the possibility I would move to Karlovac. As it turned out, that plan was soon impossible. Suljo was transferred from Karlovac to Pula, also in Croatia, but not such an appealing place to live. Along the way, he decided against becoming an officer. Still, we kept our plans to return to Karlovac and The Korana for our honeymoon.

By the time Suljo came back home after finishing his year of military service, it was clear that many things were changing around us. Though we still planned to get married, we had to rethink many of our expectations. Communism was unraveling and the economy went with it. Inflation soared. It was very hard to find work and even young people who had just graduated from the university often couldn't find jobs. All of this was new, as was the emerging black market. People scrambled to find some way to make a living.

Once more, I had scarcely welcomed Suljo home before he had to leave again. He had been out of the army for only a few weeks and we had just been swimming at the river when he said, "Jasmina, I think I'm going to have to go to France. I can get a job there again."

I was silent. It wouldn't be fair for me to protest. I knew how hard it was to find a job in Visegrad and it was true that we shouldn't start our married life penniless.

"It wouldn't be for long," he said.

"It's summer," I told him. "It's the best time of year and I want to share it with you. And you just got back." Then, more quietly, I said, "I know it's for the best. But here we are, getting ready to say goodbye again."

"I won't leave before the summer is over," he promised. "This will be your last year in school so when I come back with some money, we'll get married. How does an April wedding sound?"

It sounded fine, but I was still sad. The last weeks of summer were painfully short and a morning in September found me waiting with Suljo once again for the bus that would take him away from me.

"What should I bring you from France?"

"You," I said. "You're all I want."

"Don't be like that."

"But there's nothing I want."

"Come on, you clothes horse," he teased. "I'm talking about France. Have you heard of Paris, the fashion capital of the world? What do you want?"

"Cowboy boots," I said.

He laughed. "I knew there'd be something."

I laughed, too, but as soon as the bus left with him, I went into a deep funk. Everything seemed to conspire against us. When you're young and in love, even the obstacles that are indifferent to you seem spiteful. Yugoslavia called young men into the army just to frustrate girls like me and now the country was falling into chaos just to keep Suljo and me from the happiness we almost had in our grasp.

Even when the political situation began to grow serious, it all seemed distant compared to how much I missed Suljo. And most of the political developments were happening far away such as the people of Slovenia agitating for independence from Yugoslavia as elections approached.

Some of the nearest political developments surprised me but I had no inkling of their importance. Suddenly, people who had never talked about religion before were making a big deal of it. My homeroom teacher, Risto, emerged as president of a Serbian Orthodox party, which was hard to understand because professors weren't supposed to belong to any religious party. They were all Communists and they were always discouraging us from going to the Mosque or to church. They explained to us that school would teach us the truths we needed. "Who needed God? We had the State," they proclaimed.

I was born into a religious family, so I grew up believing in God and going to the Mosque. I also understood why Serbs went to church. I had a deep trust in the power of faith. People who believed in God, whether they sought Him in the Mosque or in church, would know they were accountable to Him for their actions. My Muslim religion taught me to be good to other people and that's why I couldn't understand why our professors discouraged religion. As far as I could see, religion made people better.

The near-sightedness of youth kept me even from seeing the

full terror of what happened next in Slovenia. When the country pressed for independence, the Yugoslav Army attacked. I knew, as everyone around me did, that this was terrible. And like everyone else, I spent hours watching the news about the war on television, trying to understand what was really happening. When Suljo pledged allegiance to the army, he and all the other young men swore to give their lives to protect the country's borders. I never dreamed that this might mean turning the army's guns on its own people.

We talked of little other than the war at first but my friends and I still had our lives to live. In some ways, Slovenia was as far from all of us as Yugoslavia was for Americans. We felt sorry for Slovenia—my friends and I had just traveled there for our senior class trip, but as the news stories from the north became less frequent and urgent, we thought of other things. Besides, we knew that what we saw on television wasn't the whole truth. The news reports said that the Slovenians had attacked the Yugoslav Army, but young soldiers from Visegrad who wrote letters home didn't remember it that way. What little we saw about the situation we thus regarded as unreliable news.

But more personal encounters were harder to ignore. The Serbian city of Belgrade held an annual exhibition of furniture from all over Yugoslavia. Naturally, everyone in my furniture design class would go each year. When my classmates and I attended, everything in Belgrade seemed to be as it had always been. My friend, Zorica, and I went to visit Kalimegdan, the prettiest part of town. As we walked on the wide streets, I began to realize that Belgrade had changed. I had a hard time paying attention to the things that I loved about Kalimegdan—there was so much history there. The city wall had been built by the Romans and had been added to, one stratum at a time, by the Celts, Turks, Austro-Hungarians and Communists. There was the Turkish bath house where you could always see gypsies dancing on the street and the mausoleum of the Turkish Beys.

But, as mentioned, I did not really see those things that time. What I noticed instead were Chetniks everywhere. They had grown long beards and every one of them wore a cap bearing the World War II Chetnik insignia. I felt them staring at me, as if they could tell just by looking that I wasn't Serbian. My hands grew clammy and Zorica noticed my concern. "Jasmina, don't worry. They're just fundamentalists."

Zorica was a Serb. We were in the same class and her house was just a few meters from my apartment building. I had grown up with her and I trusted her. But it was still hard to believe what she was telling me. I was sure that the long beards and Chetnik caps were not just signs of religious conservatism.

We went to get lunch at a McDonald's. While I waited at a table outside when Zorica went in to get our food, a boy of about twenty came up to me.

"Hey," he said, smiling, "can you help me out? My best friend is in the hospital and I want to buy him a gift but I'm broke."

It was the lamest panhandling line I'd ever heard. He was dressed well so it was obvious he wasn't poor. Then again, if he was dressed well, maybe he wasn't lying. Maybe he really did have a friend in the hospital and he was temporarily strapped for cash. I knew how that could be.

I reached into my pocket. "Here," I said, giving him some money. "I'm sorry about your friend."

My accent surprised him. His eyes narrowed and his smile vanished. "Where are you from?" he demanded.

"I'm from Visegrad, from Bosnia," I said.

"Well what the hell are you doing here?" he scowled as he pocketed my money. "This is Serbia." There was poison in his voice and he wrinkled his nose as if I were rotten garbage. I felt scared again and silently prayed for God to protect me from him. Then Zorica came out of McDonald's and he left.

"Who was that?" she asked but I just shook my head, not wanting to answer. For a long time, though, I couldn't forget the expression on his face or the hatred in his voice.

That was my last visit to Belgrade.

10

Graduation

Before long, even in Visegrad there were some Serbs who were openly hostile to Muslims. My friends were still my friends, but there were occasional demonstrations of Serbian nationalism by extremists. For the first time, I didn't feel completely safe in my own home town.

So I kept busy. Mukadesa had her hair salon inside the Hotel Vilina Vlas and I went there to work whenever I wasn't in school.

The Hotel Vilina Vlas was well known throughout Yugoslavia. It was five kilometers outside of Visegrad in the middle of the woods. A nature path surrounded the woods and next to the hotel were a few little rental houses for people who wanted to stay at Vilina Vlas for a whole season. The hotel's swimming pool was fed by a hot springs and covered in glass. Even in the depths of winter, you could lie floating on your back and see the dark silhouettes of trees all around you.

The water was special. Women who couldn't get pregnant were told to come to Vilina Vlas and many of them were said to have conceived thanks to the healing waters.

There was a grand balcony overlooking the woods, too, and there were often parties there. It was a fun place to mingle because the hotel guests came from all over Yugoslavia.

But this year, even the Vilina Vlas had changed. Guests were scarce and they kept to themselves. My sister and I were afraid to be at the hotel late at night.

And still this seemed like so much bothersome noise in the midst of a normal life. Only a month of school remained and my graduation party was coming up. A few months after that, Suljo would return from France and we'd get married. My friends and I talked mostly about what we were going to wear for our graduation party.

"So what are you wearing, Jasmina?"

"I had plans for a red dress with matching shoes but I couldn't find red shoes anywhere. I've tried three cities so far, no red shoes. So I don't know what I'll wear. What about you, Alma?"

"Nothing's right yet. I'll know what I want when I see it. Can Mukadesa do my hair?"

I had more friends than my sister had time for hair appointments. Still, I kept saying, "She'll have to fit you in. I'll be there to help her until the last minute."

Meanwhile, I went half-mad looking for those red shoes. I had been planning my outfit for months but it all started with the shoes. I couldn't very well buy the dress first, just in case the only shoes I managed to find were the wrong shade of red.

Dijana and Selma found beautiful dresses in Sarajevo but my red shoes didn't materialize. I had to give in to fate—I spent the last days before the party shopping for a black dress and matching shoes.

Mukadesa did my hair and then I helped her with my friends' hair.

Dijana, Selma and Jasmina

My graduation partner was Miodrag Bogosavljevic, who went by Jole for short. He was a Serb. That didn't bother me at all. What drove me nuts was that he was a Serb who was always late. Twenty minutes after he was supposed to pick me up, I was pacing around the apartment and looking at my watch every minute.

"Jole!" I said when he finally got there. "Why are you late?"

He sighed. "My mother wasn't home. You know I'm helpless without her."

Actually, I could have guessed. He was in a gray suit and I could tell that he'd gotten dressed without his mother's usual help. I didn't tell him so.

"Anyway, you look gorgeous!" he said.

"Thank you."

"Really, you look a lot older." We were still at the age where that was a compliment.

We were so late that when we walked down the middle of the street, we were the only couple for onlookers to see. Everyone was turning to look at us and my knees were about to buckle. I talked and talked to Jole about anything that came into my head, anything to keep my mind off the way people were looking at us. After all this effort to look great, now I was mortified that everyone was looking at me!

We arrived at the end of the street and met the other students in front of the statue of Ivo Andric, right next to the sixteenth century Na Drini Cuprija bridge.

I could breathe again. The onlookers were behind us and it was just me and my friends. Before long, we were dancing, singing and talking to each other over the music. I was laughing and having fun. The only thing missing from that perfect night was Suljo.

The party went on until morning and no one dared to go home. This was it, our last party together. We were growing up and our adult lives would lead us down different paths.

None of us imagined how sad and violent some of those paths would turn out to be.

11

―――――

Ibro

Summer – Fall 1991

At first, the war in Croatia, like the struggle in Slovenia, was a war on television. Fighting broke out days before my last high school classes. The Yugoslav Army withdrew from Slovenia and concentrated all its efforts on crushing Croatia's independence. Television showed countless bodies sprawled in the streets of Croatian towns.

Soon, however, Croatia, much more than the earlier struggles in Slovenia, struck close to home. Many young men from Visegrad were serving in the Yugoslav Army and it was impossible to get any news of them. No letters came from the young men who had previously written every week to their parents or every day to their sweethearts. Parents tried to get official news or assurances but the army could not—or would not—say whether their boys were still alive.

Nihad, Suljo's cousin, was one of the missing. His mother broke into tears whenever she thought of him—and she thought of him often. She had packed him off to join the Yugoslav Army so that he'd learn to protect us, all of us, from foreign threats. Now he was off in a neighboring republic killing some of the people he had been sworn to defend and risking death at their hands. Why?

More chilling, though, were the changes among our neighbors. Serbs sent their children to Serbia or else packed up the whole family for a trip out of the city. They didn't talk to the rest of us about what they were doing or why. They just left.

On the Muslim calendar there are two celebrations of Eid—one for the end of the Ramadan month of fasting and another to commemorate Abraham's sacrifice of a sheep instead of his son. On the second Eid of the year, our celebration of mercy and kindness, three busloads of people from Serbia drove up to the Na Drini Cuprija bridge in Visegrad. They had Chetnik flags painted on their buses and wore the Chetnik insignia on their caps: four C's linked together. The letter C is an S in the Cyrillic alphabet. The four linked C's represent the ideal of gathering all the Serbs in one Greater Serbia.

The Serbs held a rally on our bridge, waving their flags and shouting, "This is Serbia! This is Serbia!" They shouted other things, too, words full of hatred for everyone in Visegrad who wasn't Serb. They had to know that this was our holiday. The timing of their demonstration was no accident.

There were scuffles. Some Bosnians set fire to the Serbian flag. Before long, the buses were headed back to Serbia but a cloud of fear and anger hung over the city for the rest of the day. The streets were empty. The cafés closed early.

We wanted so much to believe that this was all an aberration that would pass. The next day it was as if nothing had happened. The streets were full again. Summer had arrived and the Drina River beckoned with its cool water. Days followed days and things seemed almost normal for a while. My brother, Tajib, got married. Life went on and not all the Serbs who had gone away stayed away, though many Serbian children remained in Serbia.

Suljo returned from France. He had saved some money and found a job in a Visegrad café. We could finally be together and think about our marriage.

One afternoon, Suljo called me from work. "It's a slow day here," he said. "The boss just gave me a two-hour break. Let's do something. I'll come pick you up."

I got ready and went out onto the balcony that looked out over Nova Mahala. I expected to see Suljo coming.

What I saw instead was a parade of weaponry. The Yugoslav Army and Chetnik volunteers came marching up our street. They carried rifles and machine guns—more weapons than I had seen in my life. Armored vehicles rumbled along behind the marching troops. They kept passing, rank after rank of soldiers and weapons. The Yugoslav Army was one of the world's largest.

The Chetniks in the ranks of regular soldiers made it clear. Our national army was now a Chetnik army.

That alone might have made me shiver. Chetniks, the monstrous people of my grandparents' stories, the people who, like the fairy tale monsters of childhood, I had relegated to a distant past, were not only very real—they were marching in Visegrad.

Worse, far worse, was the reaction of my Serbian neighbors. People I had grown up with, gone to school with, the adults I had looked up to, they were on the street clapping their hands and cheering the Chetniks on. Tanja was out there. Dragana was. They were my friends but they were applauding the soldiers who were on their way to kill our fellow Yugoslavs in Croatia.

I saw Suljo making his way up the street and I went out to meet him.

For a long time, we just watched the soldiers going by. "How long is it going to take them to march through Visegrad?" Suljo said. "How many of them can there be?" Tanks and trucks rumbled by, followed by artillery pieces.

They kept coming for much longer than we'd imagined they might. Suljo's two-hour break ended and he went back to work. Still, the army marched by. Night fell. And still, the soldiers and Chetniks came while the Serbs called encouragement to them from the sides of the street.

Now and then I would catch the gaze of Serbs I knew. In the eyes of some of them, I saw shadows of the hate that I'd seen in the eyes of that boy in Belgrade, the one who had asked me for money.

When the Muslim party won in the Bosnian elections, the gaze of those neighbors grew darker still.

Things got worse. One evening, as I was getting ready to go out with Suljo, the telephone rang.

"Hello?"

"Jasmina? Is that you?" It was Meliha, Alma's sister. "Why aren't you at your uncle's house?" There was something strange in her voice.

"Why should I be there? What's going on?"

"There are a lot of people gathered out front."

Oh no, I thought. My uncle had a heart attack or something.

But Meliha said, "I think your cousin Ibro has been killed." My legs felt stuck to the floor as I opened my mouth once or twice without saying anything. *Ibro, dead? Killed?*

I hung up the phone and told my sister Amira what Meliha had said. Then I called Suljo and we went together to my uncle's house.

The place was packed with people. Some were crying. Others looked bewildered. My uncle was screaming—his face was red and wet.

Ibro's wife and son arrived at the same time we did. They had just come from Sarajevo to visit her parents but she had come over because she hadn't heard from her husband when she expected to.

My uncle told her that Ibro was dead and she fainted. Bit by bit, I began to hear the story. Ibro and three friends—a man and two women—had driven into Croatia. The women went for a swim while Ibro and his friend, Medo, went into a store to buy some things. When they returned from shopping, Ibro opened the door of the car and it exploded, killing them instantly.

The version that soon appeared in the Serb-controlled press was that Ibro and Medo were Muslim extremists whose own bomb had blown them up by mistake. People tended to believe what they read and we had a hard time convincing anyone who didn't know him that Ibro simply wouldn't be involved in such a thing. We hoped that the two women could shed some light on the matter, but they had disappeared.

When Ibro and Medo's families went to claim the bodies which had been sent to Montenegro, the police there treated them like animals. They returned very frightened.

At the funeral, attended by hundreds, only four Serbs showed up. Even my uncle's best friends, who were Serbs, didn't show.

It was months later that the two women surfaced again. They had been jailed by the Serbs and tortured. They were convinced that the Serbs themselves had planted the bomb and manufactured the story about Ibro and Medo's terrorist intentions. By then, there were other such stories, enough so that there was a clear pattern: supposed Muslim terrorists frequently became scapegoats for their own murders.

Croatian refugees poured into Bosnia—often with nothing but the clothes on their backs—having witnessed horrifying stories of atrocities. They told us that Bosnia wasn't safe, either, that the Serbs would turn their guns on us soon enough.

That scared us. We had nothing but hunting rifles with which to protect ourselves.

My brother, Azem, and his friend, Ibrahim, were among those who took the danger very seriously. They went to Croatia to train with the Croatians. They weren't alone. Perhaps five thousand Bosnians joined the fight on Croatian soil against the Yugoslav Army.

Some of the Visegrad boys who had served in the Yugoslav Army began to turn up again. Nihad was one who had managed to escape the army. He wasn't the boy I once knew. Nihad was in a daze all the time with a zombie stare. At first, he wouldn't talk about his experiences but then he began to recount the deaths of his friends in the army. The Serbian officers sang songs that glorified a Greater Serbia while those under their command had to sit and listen. Then the officers sent Bosnian boys to fight the Croats and many of them died.

But the urge for a normal life is like a buoy that you try to sink in a river. You push it down but it pops back up to the surface. Even Nihad lost his zombie stare after a few weeks.

12

Love & Celebration

December 1991 – January 1992

Our own lives were thankfully able to often distract us from what was happening around us. In December, Mukadesa got married and Azem and Ibrahim came to visit us for a few days. It was great to see them after such a long time. New Year's was just around the corner and friends who were studying away from Visegrad would be returning home for the parties. My hometown was in many respects the place it had always been. We left war out of our conversations. It was a time for fun and celebration. A blanket of snow covered the ground and Visegrad was lit up at night like a Christmas tree. Suljo and I took long walks in the snow, enjoying the lights and the people busy celebrating on the streets.

When Suljo and I had a snowball fight, I felt that the bad times really were going to pass, that Visegrad would be as it had always been.

But there was a change in the New Year's parties that year.

In Bosnia, we always celebrated the New Year with three or four nights of singing and dancing and often we wouldn't sleep much in between. That year, the parties were, if anything, more energetic than in most years.

By the morning of the fourth day—January 4th, 1992—I could hardly move. I was danced out. When I dragged myself out of bed, I made some coffee and started to dial Dijana. Then the doorbell rang. Samir went to see who it was.

"Suljo's waiting for you," he said.

So early? I thought. I went to the balcony in my pajamas. Why was Suljo's father with him?

"Jasmina, can you come down?"

"Let me dress!"

I threw on my jeans and was on my way down when Suljo met me on the stairs.

"Jasmina, will you marry me? Today?"

I didn't know what to say. We'd been planning on an April wedding, or March at the earliest. I was surprised but found that I was grinning, too. I wanted Suljo more than anything in the world.

"Well, say something," he said. "I already told my parents and my neighbors that we're getting married today." He was smiling, too.

"Yes, of course I want to marry you!"

He threw his arms around me and there were tears of happiness in his eyes. If anything could be a sign that everything was going to be all right, wasn't this it? I didn't stop to think that Suljo might believe that time was running out for us.

Telling the news to my friends was fun. I made a game of it when, a few minutes after Suljo and his father had gone, the phone rang. It was Sabina, calling from her family's store.

"Hey, Dijana and I are waiting for you. When are you coming?"

"Oh, Sabina. I'm sorry. I can't come today."

"Why not? How was the party you went to last night?"

"The party was good."

"Just come here for a few minutes."

"But I'm so busy."

"Oh, cut it out. Come see us."

"Well, just to say goodbye."

"Say goodbye?"

"Yes, I'm getting married today. Suljo and I are going to Sarajevo."

There was a long silence on the other end of the line. I wish I could have seen Sabina's face.

"I've got to go," I told her. "I haven't told my mother yet. 'Bye!"

I knew that Sabina and Dijana would go crazy with wanting to hear all the details. I really wanted to talk to them, too, but I also had to get my nerve up to talk to my mother. I packed, then paced around the apartment, trying to think of what I would say.

I felt a little sad for her, really. Mukadesa had just gotten married. Azem had been away for a long time and Tajib had a house of his own and a wife who was pregnant. My mother would stay alone in the house all day now with the younger children. It would be a lot of work for her without us older kids around to pitch in. Not that she would think about the work. What she would say was that she missed having all of us together.

"Mama," I said at last. "I need to talk to you."

"Do you need money?"

"No, Mama. I don't need money."

"Are you going somewhere?"

"To Sarajevo, Mama." Then the words spilled out in a rush. "Suljo and I want to get married today."

Her face was happy and sad at the same time, just as I knew it would be. After today, I'd be expected to treat my in-laws as my mother and father. Suljo and I would live with them until we could afford a place of our own—that's often how it was in Bosnia. I was going to leave home today and become the daughter of another household.

"Jasmina," my mother said. "This is sudden! You told me you were getting married in April." She looked into my eyes and smiled. "When are you going?"

"In three hours. Mama, Suljo and I will come to help you whenever we can. You know how much Suljo loves you. You'll be gaining a son."

About then, Selma came. She had heard the news from Suljo. Like my mother, she was happy for me, but knew she was losing me, too.

"Jasmina, you didn't tell me about this. When did you and Suljo decide?"

"I'm sorry, Selma. I wasn't keeping any secrets from you. Suljo asked this morning and I said yes."

The doorbell rang. Selma went to answer it and my mother took the opportunity to give me some last-minute advice. She told me to listen to Suljo. I was to refer to Suljo's mother as my mother and treat his parents as I would treat my own mother and father. Visegrad, she reminded me, was a small city. People knew everything and she didn't want to hear any rumors that her daughter wasn't respectful of her in-laws.

She had more to say but there wasn't time. Selma was saying, "Suljo! Why are you stealing her from us?" She kept teasing him and Suljo looked a little bashful when he came in. "I'm not stealing her," he said. "After we return from Sarajevo, you can visit her anytime you like."

"We're happy for you," Selma said more seriously. "You're a great couple. I hope I'll have a love like yours someday."

Selma wasn't lucky in love. She had often told me how grateful I should be for a man like Suljo. And I was. Suljo had a great heart and he got along with everyone. People liked him and I loved him with all my soul.

"My children," my mother said as we left, "may you have the best of everything in your lives." She was crying. "Listen to each other. Jasmina, call me from Sarajevo!"

"Take care, Mama!"

There were hugs all around and more tears. And this was just the beginning of our leave-takings.

I went to the apartments where my grandfather lived. Ever since World War II, he had tried to keep all the family living together in one place. During the war, they'd been separated during the fighting. Fleeing Visegrad, my grandfather had been shot in the arm by a Chetnik sniper. He had been carrying my father, who was about two years old, across the Na Drini Cuprija bridge. But with his wound my grandfather couldn't hold my father any longer. He had to hide him under a gutted tank at the end of the bridge. My Aunt Hanumica went back, braving Chetnik bullets herself, to carry my father into the relative safety of the woods. Another aunt had died as the family walked to Sarajevo through five days of bitter cold and snow. In Sarajevo, my grandmother died. After that, my grandfather had pledged to keep the family in one spot. And he had been successful. My grandfather's children and grandchildren all lived in the same apartment building with him. All, that is, but my father and us, and we lived only a block away.

So when Suljo and I went to that building to say goodbye to Tajib, it was a mob scene.

"My Mince is getting married?" Tajib said. Mince was one of his nicknames for me. He hardly ever called me Jasmina, unless I had borrowed his motorcycle or something. "This makes two sisters in a month," he went on. "I hope Amira isn't getting married!"

I laughed. Boyfriends were still the furthest thing from her mind.

As we talked, the news spread and the apartment building emptied.

"It's true that you're still very young, Jasmina," said my Aunt Munevera. "But now that I see who your husband is going to be, I can see why you don't want to wait. You look great together. I never knew that Suljo was so handsome and nice."

Suljo's face grew red and it only grew redder as more of my aunts, uncles and cousins came into the courtyard. I should have warned him that this would happen. You couldn't come to this building and talk to just one member of my family.

Everyone was hugging and kissing Suljo and giving us money. I kept saying that I wasn't a child now, that they didn't need to give me money, but they said things like, "It's a big city, you'll need more," or "Take it just in case. You never know. Extra money is a good idea away from home."

It had been our dream to honeymoon in Karlovac at The Korana where we had stayed after his army allegiance ceremony. But the same army that Suljo had pledged to serve had shelled the city mercilessly. The hotel had been destroyed.

Sarajevo was a fine place for a wedding and honeymoon, anyway. We met Suljo's grandmother in Buca Potok, a suburb just outside the city. She gave me a big welcome-to-the-family hug and then she commenced an endless string of jokes. She was very funny. Though she was sixty-five years old, in many ways she acted like my friends.

She had cared for Suljo when he was little and in some ways Suljo was five years old whenever he was with her. He would put his head on her lap and she would comfort him like a baby, all the while keeping up her string of jokes. We laughed a lot in her company.

Suljo and I were married in a civil ceremony—the way almost everyone had been married in Communist Yugoslavia. Then we went to a ski mountain called Johorina for our honeymoon. The mountain overlooked Sarajevo. The hotels there were beautiful and those first days of my marriage were the best of my life. Suljo woke me every day to tell me how much in love with me he was and all day long he told me over and over how happy he was. We were mirrors for each other's happiness.

But even on these happiest of days, we could feel the ground shifting beneath our feet. On the ski mountain, there were a lot of army units with tanks and artillery. People would ask each other what they were doing there. But they were still our army. We were still part of Yugoslavia. Here, the disquieting Chetnik insignia wasn't much in evidence. And, of course, people were busy skiing and playing. There on Johorina, fear and black thoughts seemed out of place.

13

Perfect Rice

March 1992

After the honeymoon, back in Visegrad, Suljo's family welcomed me into their household. It was an uncomfortable transition for me—new house, new parents, new neighbors. Whenever I went out, I felt that everyone was looking at me. I hated the feeling that I was an outsider in the place I had come to live. But Suljo's mother could not have been more understanding.

Things got easier. One by one, the neighbors came to meet me. Day by day, more people greeted me by name whenever I went out. Suljo's parents truly seemed to think of me as their daughter and I soon loved them as I loved my own mother and father.

I still had one big problem. I didn't know how to cook. Since I was the only one who stayed home all day while Suljo and his parents went out to work, it made sense that I should have dinner waiting for them when they returned. But in my mother's house, I only cleaned house, washed the dishes and looked after my siblings. My mother always cooked because all of us kids were always at school, at work or playing sports. We hardly ever stayed in the apartment long enough to cook something.

Suljo's grandmother came to Visegrad with us from Sarajevo and she taught me how to bake bread and cook a few dishes. But when she returned home, I only knew how to cook the dishes she had taught me and they weren't enough.

I got in the habit of calling my mother. She'd stay on the phone with me, going over how to make something step-by-step and we wouldn't hang up until the dish was done. But there's a fine touch to cooking and I didn't have it yet. It takes experience to know how hot is too hot, which spices don't go together. Sometimes you get experience by burning the stew onto the bottom of the pot or mixing ginger and sage. Suljo's father would always say, no matter what I put before him at dinner, "This is very good!"

Too often, this was a kind-hearted lie. But he ate everything. And that helped. I felt bad that I couldn't get in the saucepan the results that were in my heart. Suljo's parents were so loving to me and I wanted to please them.

One day when Suljo was also home from work, my mother-in-law told me that she'd love to have chicken with rice for dinner when she came home. I didn't know how to cook that and neither did Suljo.

"Mama," I said over the phone, "can you please tell me how to cook chicken with rice?"

Step-by-step, she explained how to prepare the dish. I wrote down the instructions and Suljo and I spent the day assembling the ingredients and cooking. But when we had finished, the rice tasted bad.

By then, Suljo's parents were due home in an hour. In a panic, I called my mother again.

"I did everything just as you said," I told her. "The rice is terrible."

"Maybe you didn't put enough water into the pan," she said.

"How can I tell without tasting the rice?"

So I tried to explain to her the consistency and taste of the rice. I went over all the instructions I had written down earlier. Then we started it all over, trying to figure out what had gone wrong. She knew how much I wanted to please my in-laws.

Finally, Suljo took the phone from me. "Mama," he said into the receiver, "it would be cheaper to eat in a restaurant. Whenever Jasmina cooks something she spends the day on the phone with you and I have to pay the phone bill!"

My mother laughed. She told Suljo we should just try the rice again with a little more water. This time the rice was finished just before Suljo's mother walked in the door.

At the stove, my mother-in-law said, "Wow, Jasmina! Rice can be tricky and this is perfect. I don't think I've made more perfect rice myself!"

Suljo and I broke up laughing but we wouldn't tell her what was so funny.

"The key to perfect rice," Suljo later whispered to me, "is to make it all day long!"

"Perfect rice" was our private joke after that. Suljo was sweet, though. He never told my mother-in-law the whole story.

14

Everything Changes

The first three months of our marriage seemed more like three days to me. Soon, April arrived with its sunshine. We welcomed the new season but it was a disquieting spring. It was the month Suljo and I had planned to have a belated wedding reception but we canceled those plans. Suljo's sister in Austria couldn't come because of the war in Croatia. His family in France couldn't come, either. In fact, even if they had made it into Bosnia safely, traffic on both sides of Visegrad had been shut down at Serbian checkpoints. Bosnian cities near the Serbian border were being systematically cut off.

Everything felt increasingly dangerous. Serbs on the police force in Visegrad deserted the city, taking their weapons with them into the surrounding hills.

More Serbs left Visegrad. The population and local economy seemed to shrink overnight. My in-laws were soon working much shorter hours. Serbs didn't come to work at all and the

Serbian children who were still in town didn't go to school. Suljo closed the café earlier and earlier. Soon, the city was dead quiet every night by ten.

I started to remember the stories of my grandparents, the tales of Chetniks coming to Visegrad to rape and kill and burn.

Nonetheless, I imagined that somehow I was safe because I had grown up with Serbs and still counted many of them as my friends. Chetniks were extremists from far away. I could rely on my neighbors.

People old enough to remember the last time, though, were very afraid. Older residents of Visegrad were putting extra food aside and packing clothes so that they could leave at a moment's notice.

"You children don't know who the Chetniks are," they had always told us, "but we know them very well."

Of course, we had seen Chetniks doing terrible things in old war movies. But it still seemed hard to believe that anyone could really be a Chetnik in 1992. They might be Serbian extremists, but I couldn't imagine that they would want to destroy us just because we weren't Serbs.

Especially then, in April, it was easy to remember how well we had always gotten along. It was Eid, the holiday following Ramadan. In the past, Serbs had always celebrated our holiday with us. They came to visit us and ate our Eid cake. I would always bring some cake to our cafés for the waiters.

The first day of Eid was for visiting family. Suljo and I dressed up and went to see my mother before anyone else, as was the tradition. She had baked the usual cakes and my younger brothers greeted us happily. The day was also special for children because they could expect gifts of money from all of the adults in the family. They waited for that day as eagerly as kids in America wait for Christmas.

But my mother's cheer was forced. Tajib's wife, Rukija, arrived in equally gloomy spirits. She immediately went out onto the balcony, with her back to the sounds of the children's voices. She seemed to be looking at something far away.

I went to join her. I wanted to ask what was wrong but I didn't know what to say. Finally, she spoke first.

"I haven't heard from Tajib in three days."

I was shocked. Suljo and I had been expecting Tajib to come through the door at any moment.

"Where is he?"

Rukija nodded at the distant hills. "He's in Dobrun. The Yugoslav Army and the Chetniks started to shoot into Dobrun. Soon they'll do the same to us. Tajib and some others went to defend Dobrun. Bahe is there, too."

I couldn't say anything. I couldn't move.

Dobrun was a large village on the border with Serbia. By car, it was only half an hour from my mother's apartment.

Finally, I understood why the Serbs had been leaving Visegrad. *Why hadn't any of the Serbs come to my father's door, as friends, to warn us? Why did our friends abandon us without at least telling us what they thought might happen? "Listen, Nurko," they might have said, "there are rumors. Things are going to get bad. As your friend, I'm telling you to get your family out of here..." They weren't Chetniks. We'd always lived together in peace. The Eid cake there on the table had always been shared with them. That, and more. Our lives were intertwined.*

"Women and children have been escaping from Dobrun," Rukija went on. "They had to flee through the woods. A woman from Dobrun and her child slept last night in our house. I invited her here. She'll come soon."

Rukija was still looking into the distance.

"She can't stop shaking. It's terrible, the way she trembles." I wanted to know more but my sister-in-law's face was white. I took her hand and led her back inside the apartment.

I exchanged a look with my mother but we said nothing.

"I should be there, too," Suljo said. "With Tajib, protecting Dobrun."

I hadn't known he was listening.

When the woman from Dobrun arrived, though, we realized from her story that there was nothing left to protect. She looked ill, as if she'd just been released from the hospital. She hardly had the energy to stand and fell into a chair at once.

"I can't explain to you how it is," she said. "If you've never been through something like this, you won't be able to imagine it."

There were shadows under her eyes. My mother asked if she wanted something to eat or drink. She really looked as if she might pass out but she shook her head.

"We ran seven kilometers through the woods with our children. All the time, Chetniks and soldiers were screaming at us, shooting in our direction. Once we had gone a little ways from the village, shells started to explode around us. I had clothes for the children, but I dropped them. We had to hurry."

"Did everyone get out? Did you all escape?"

"I don't know. I couldn't stop to look around. The shells were falling. We just ran for our lives. The men stayed behind but what can they do? They have guns that shoot one bullet at a time. The army has tanks and planes. We're ants to them."

This is not my world, I thought. *I live in 1992. This is not my grandparents' time.*

The woman showed us the cuts and bruises she had from running through the woods. Her child started to scream. "At least we're alive," she said.

The phone rang. It was my father-in-law.

"Jasmina," he said, "I'm coming to pick you up. You and Suljo must come home immediately. The situation is bad."

His fear in his voice scared me.

"Yes, we'll be ready."

I wanted to ask Rukija to tell me more about Tajib but there wasn't time. We wished good luck to my mother, my sister-in-law and the woman from Dobrun. I grasped Suljo's hand as we went downstairs. At least I would always have him, I thought. He made me feel safe and secure even as everything was falling apart.

"We won't sleep at home," Suljo's father said as we got into the car. When we get home, pack your things. We'll sleep at Hajra's house." Hajra was Suljo's aunt, mother to his cousin Nihad, who had fought for the army in Croatia.

We stayed with Hajra that night, but none of us slept. The women stayed up talking in low voices. I finally understood the urgency of Suljo's father. Two thousand Chetniks were massed outside Visegrad. There were army units with them, with heavy guns.

The men patrolled the streets. Everyone who had a hunting rifle had taken it out and cleaned it. But what good could hunting rifles do against a modern army?

Finally, I left the other women and went to lie down. Suljo came to see me and he didn't have good news.

"Some people have come from Dobrun," he said. "It's crazy there. Shells are raining down on what's left of the village. The defenders agreed to get out. All but a few. Tajib and his friends are still there. They refuse to pull back."

"Is he crazy?" I made my hands into fists. "He'll die there!" I understood that someone had to try to defend us. I even knew the sort of thing that Tajib would be thinking, that to give way was, sooner or later, to give up. But the situation in Dobrun sounded hopeless.

I asked Suljo questions but he had already told me everything he knew.

The next day brought us news that we thought would be our salvation. The United States of America had recognized Bosnia's independence. With U.S. recognition, we were confident that all the world would now see us as a nation—the world's youngest nation. We were no longer part of Yugoslavia, no longer part of the country that was massacring civilians in Croatia. Surely, the Serbs would see that their hopes for expanding Serbia were futile. We would have peace.

That's not how the Serbs saw things.

That day, the sniper fire from the hills around Visegrad began. More news came to us that day by word of mouth. Arkan, a Serb officer who was quickly gaining a reputation for his brutality, had overrun the cities of Bijeljina and Zvornik. Zvornik, like Visegrad, was a city on the Drina but closer to Serbia.

It was said that Arkan's troops were raping women and girls, even very young girls. Anyone who showed the slightest resistance was killed on the spot. There were Chetniks shooting people in Foca, too.

Our brief glimmer of hope had quickly turned to fear. There were bodies floating in the Drina not far from Visegrad. That's what I heard. I didn't see them myself, but it wasn't hard to believe. The current was carrying some of the dead from Zvornik and Foca to the reservoir above our city.

In those hours of waiting for the big guns to open up on us, people hatched desperate plans. One man who tried to stop the Serbs was Murat Sabanovic, Sabina's uncle. He tried to get the Serbs to back down by threatening to destroy everything that we imagined would make Visegrad worth taking.

The hydroelectric dam in Visegrad generated power for our city and others. It also held back many tons of water. Sabina's Uncle Murat knew that the Serbs would want to take the power station intact and he threatened to make that impossible if they didn't stop shooting into Visegrad. He said he had planted explosives in the dam.

The power station and dam were huge. It had take seven thousand construction workers six years to build it. Blowing it up would black out the region. It would also destroy Visegrad and other cities downstream. What good would Visegrad be to the Serbs if it were under water? What would they have won?

A few of us learned that the threat was a bluff. Murat Sabanovic certainly had the know-how to demolish the dam and the Serbs knew it. What he lacked was the necessary explosives. Whether the Serbs knew that or not, we weren't sure.

Murat invited the whole city to come to the dam for a show of unity. He proclaimed that we'd rather blow ourselves sky high and leave a watery scar on Bosnia than die a humiliating, helpless death at the hands of our own army. There was an army barracks near the dam and Murat said the explosion would take those soldiers with us.

People came. First it was the people of Dusce. Then others. Then still more. Soon the dam was swarming with the people of Visegrad. It was a chaotic scene and a little surreal. People came with blankets and pillows and the food they had made for the Eid holiday.

I called my mother. She didn't know that the dam didn't have real explosives and I didn't dare reassure her over the phone. She told me that they were going to escape to Bikavac, a hill overlooking Visegrad. Bikavac was the site of a beautiful hotel and gardens. It used to be a retreat for lovers. Now it was a retreat for people who were fleeing for their lives. People went there because it would be safe from the flood waters.

Many people spent the night on the dam. The next day, Murat Sabanovic's threat to blow it up was national news. All of Bosnia's eyes and ears were turned to our city. There were television uplinks for Murat and the country watched as the Bosnian President, Alija Izetbegovic, and General Kukanjac of the Yugoslav Army pleaded with Murat not to go through with his plan. Murat was convincing. I wondered if he really had managed to secure the necessary explosives.

But the troops on the hills above Visegrad and in the barracks near the dam weren't convinced. Either that, or they simply didn't care what we did. They started sniping at the people on the dam. Soon, the shelling of Visegrad began.

Most of us had never seen artillery shells exploding except in the movies. In all my life, I've never been as terrified as I was in that first barrage. I understood then why the woman who had escaped Dobrun could not stop shaking. I could feel the explosive shock waves in the ground under my feet. I could feel them in my guts.

Again, I wondered why none of our Serbian friends had warned us. Or why hadn't they stood up for us and stayed in Visegrad? The Serbs wouldn't attack the city if it were still full of Serbs, would they?

Even as the shells were falling, the debate between Murat Sabanovic, the Bosnian President, and the Serbian General continued on the television. Murat said that he could hardly keep up the dialogue while the Yugoslav Army was shelling civilians in the city.

General Kukanjac insisted that if someone was shelling the city, it was just some unit of out-of-control irregulars. He promised that he'd stop them.

It was an absurd suggestion. Ragtag Chetnik units didn't have artillery. Only the Army could drop shells on our heads.

The television exchange grew even more bizarre. Murat's sister was brought to the television station in Sarajevo and over the airwaves she tearfully begged her brother not to do what he was contemplating.

The television debate, though, was only a sideshow. It didn't actually slow the tanks coming from Titovo Uzice or the Chetniks advancing from the hills. Murat's bluff was being called and the only thing for us to do was flee.

Suljo and I went with his parents to our apartment. I was numb. I sat in the car as they rushed around. My in-laws came out to me.

"Jasmina, you'll need clothes," my father-in-law said. I still didn't move.

"War or no war, you have to wear something," said my mother-in-law.

"Mama, I'm sick. I don't want anything. I don't need anything." I started to cry. War was here. I would never want, never need anything again.

They put their clothes as well as some of mine into the car. They packed blankets and food, including the baklava that Suljo's mother had made for Eid.

What do refugees eat? I can tell you. They eat baklava. Suljo sat beside me and tried to reassure me but the exploding shells were louder than his words. Suljo's father started the car and soon we were on the road that led out of town. No one stopped us. Visegrad's streets were deserted, the Drina looked cold and gray. The city of my childhood was a dark city. Already, it looked half-dead.

15

Visegrad Refugees

Our first place of refuge was a small hilltop village not far from Visegrad. It overlooked the Drina and you could even see most of Visegrad from there. Somewhere on the opposite side of the river were my parents. I prayed that they had made it out of the city safely.

The village was Muslim. Serbs lived in the next village over. That was the way it had long been in the countryside. The people in neighboring villages knew each other but they didn't intermarry or mix as casually as they did in the larger towns and cities. Many Chetnik leaders and nationalist Serbs, men like Slobodan Molosevic, grew up in villages which might partly explain how their thinking developed as it did.

The people who opened their house to us were an elderly couple. We were strangers to them yet they welcomed about twenty of us Visegrad refugees. Their dinner table was so small that we had to eat in shifts. All the time, we could hear the distant sounds of the shelling.

On our second or third night with them, the couple told Suljo and me how their life together had started out like ours. Like us, they had married just at the outbreak of war. The man had left home to join the fight against the German occupation and the woman stayed with his parents. The fighting often went badly for the ragtag Yugoslav forces. They fought a guerrilla war which meant that they were always on the move. Months turned to years and there was no word from the husband. His parents finally said that he must have been killed and they told the woman to return to her own parents and forget about him. She should get on with her life, they said.

She went back to her parents but she never gave up hoping that she'd see her husband alive one day. At the war's end, she was on her way to visit her in-laws to ask if any word had come. Nearing their house, who did she see coming from the other direction but her husband. After four years of war, he was finally coming home. They embraced in front of his parents' home and were never apart again.

"And now, young couple," the old woman said with a smile, "we will show you to your room." She and the old man led the way to their bedroom. "This is where you'll sleep tonight." Suljo and I started to protest. This was a small house. Almost everyone else was sleeping on the floor somewhere, packed shoulder to shoulder as they had been at the hydroelectric station.

"This is your room tonight," the old woman insisted. And after hearing the story of their long separation, Suljo and I knew that we should accept, that the future might hold anything.

We stayed in the room but we didn't sleep. Suljo and I talked in low voices about what was happening around us. I was worried about my family. Where were they? In Bikavac, as they had planned? Suljo hoped that Tajib wasn't still in Dobrun. Did he pull back to Visegrad at last, as the other defenders had done?

We both had the same questions and neither of us had any answers to offer. But talking made us feel better. Suljo was that kind of man—it was easy for him to pour out his heart.

Finally, when we had asked the answerless questions countless times, we both began to drift off to sleep.

That's when gunfire and explosions erupted in the woods. Suljo and I sat up. There was a commotion in the house and a loud thwack from somewhere. We later discovered that a stray bullet had ended up in the bathroom.

"They have a lot of weapons," the old man was explaining when we got up to investigate. He was talking about the Serbs in the next village. "Machine guns and hand grenades. We didn't want to alarm you."

The Serbs were still deep in the woods and they didn't get near the house that night. But in the morning, everyone bustled about under the old woman's direction. She had been through one war and she knew what to do. She and the other women baked lots of bread and hurried to hide it, along with other food, in many places inside the house and out in the yard.

"If the Chetniks burn the house," she explained, "at least some of the food will be safe in the yard. If we're lucky, they'll only loot and the food in the house will be safe. But you can't count on that. We'll be able to sneak back here at night and at least find something to eat."

"Why would they burn the house?" I asked.

"Because they are Chetniks," the woman answered. "They did it in World War II and so I expect they'll do it again."

Her husband watched the preparations without expression.

"I'm not going to run," he said. "I had to escape from here when I was a young man but I'm too old for that nonsense now."

His wife tried to change his mind but he refused to even consider leaving. "I want to die in my house," he said.

And he stayed behind when all the rest of us went to sleep that night in the woods. It would be safer, everyone agreed, because the Chetniks couldn't kill us if they couldn't find us.

It was windy that night in the forest. The trees swayed in the wind and it sounded all the time as if someone were out there among the branches coming toward us.

The children were afraid. I don't know which fear was worse—theirs, for not knowing what was going on, or ours, for knowing very well what might happen next. Mothers kept feeding the young ones to keep them from crying. It was cold. The children finally fell asleep in their mothers' arms.

We all huddled close in our blankets. We didn't talk.

At one point, I was sure that I heard movement in the woods. And then there were voices. I listened and I could tell it was other people from the village hiding out like us. I wanted to call them over to us because I felt safer with more people. "No," the old woman insisted. "It's better that we stay in small groups."

I began to shiver uncontrollably. My mother-in-law gave Suljo another blanket. "Cover Jasmina. Can't you see how she's shaking?" But I don't know if it was the cold that was affecting me or fear.

Suljo put the blanket over me and hugged me close. I stopped shaking. My eyelids grew heavy. The wind had died down some so that the leaves only rustled in the trees. I dozed.

And woke suddenly. There was a rumble like an earthquake. I could feel the ground shake beneath me and everyone was standing up, looking toward the source of the sound.

In the half light, we could see distant Visegrad. The rumble was the Drina River, white and huge and angry.

Murat Sabanovic had done the only thing he could to fulfill

his threat. He didn't have explosives but he controlled the dam. He had pulled the turbines and set the Drina free. My beloved river looked like an uncaged creature, furious that it had ever been restrained. The river's roar lasted for an hour. Then, almost as suddenly, the sound was gone.

Only with the full light of morning and from the top of a nearby hill could we see the extent of the devastation. Houses that had stood on the river banks were under water. The apartment that Suljo and I shared with his parents was half submerged. Some buildings had been swept away. Even the Sports Center had been claimed by the Drina.

Something changed inside me as Suljo and I stood gazing at our flooded city. In a funny way, I wasn't afraid any longer. I realized then how bad things were in Bosnia. This was only the beginning. There was nothing I could do to stop the destruction.

The only way for me to survive was to be strong. I couldn't cry any more. Tears were wasted. Tears didn't keep the shells from falling. We were all going to need each other and we had better all be strong. I couldn't fall apart as I had in Visegrad, just sitting there in the car, numb.

People in the village were clearing out. We watched them, unsure if they knew any better than we did where it was safe to go from there. Finally, as the village began to feel like a ghost town, all of us who had been staying in the house packed up our cars and followed.

We didn't know where we were going. It just made sense not to be the only ones left behind. When we got to the main road, it was choked with traffic. All the Muslims in Visegrad were fleeing. Trucks and buses were packed with people who had no other way to travel.

My father-in-law saw a friend of his and hailed him. They got out of their cars to talk.

"Where's everybody going?" my father-in-law asked. "We were out of Visegrad these last few days. What's been happening?"

The other man began to weep. He kept turning his head as if he were looking for something in the nearby vehicles. Finally, he told my father-in-law that Dobrun had fallen. The Drina was full of corpses from Uzice. Heavy trucks driven by Serbs had been passing through the city. The trucks stank, full of bodies from Dobrun.

"The smell of the dead is everywhere in Visegrad," he said. "It seeps into the cracks. I was in Dobrun for five days looking for my wife and my children. I still haven't found them. Everybody's going to Gorazde."

"I don't know if we can make it to Gorazde," said my father-in-law. "We don't have enough gas."

It was a big problem in Bosnia even before the war. Gas was scarce. Actually, the car we were driving in had enough gas, but my father-in-law was speaking for the families who were with us. He didn't want to leave anyone behind.

"I have some gas," said his friend. "It is yours. Take it." I wanted to ask the man if he knew anything about my brother, Tajib, but he was so distraught that I left him alone.

I hadn't had any word from my family in days.

When we arrived at a village between Visegrad and Gorazde, I saw a few of my friends. Among them was Dijana's boyfriend, Edo. Actually, my mother-in-law saw him first. "There's Edo," she said. "I just know he'll have cigarettes." She had run out days ago.

"I don't know about Tajib," he said in answer to my questions as he shared his cigarettes with my mother-in-law. "But the rest of your family was going to Gorazde from Bikavac."

"Are you sure?"

"It's what I heard, but who can be sure?"

"You saved my life, Edo," my mother-in-law said, lighting one of the cigarettes.

"And Dijana?" I asked. "Do you know where she is?"

"She and Selma and their families went to Gorazde. Everybody's going to Gorazde."

I was so happy. I was ready to lose everything so long as my friends and my family were all right. Now if I could only have some news of Tajib.

16

Reunion in Gorazde

Gorazde was a little bigger than Visegrad and when the roads weren't choked with refugees, it was only a twenty-minute drive away. I'd often gone there for sports competitions and to hang out with my friends. I knew the cafés of Gorazde as well as I did the ones in Visegrad.

Those cafés were crammed full of people. Everything looked normal, though more crowded than usual. We were too far from Visegrad to hear the shelling.

The people of Gorazde opened their hearts and their homes to the refugees from Visegrad and Foca. They turned their Sports Center into a processing center for us and found a place to sleep for everyone. Gorazde families were each taking in two or three other families, usually people who were complete strangers.

We stopped the car at the Sports Center. I got out and saw lots of familiar faces from home. I looked around for someone who might have news about Tajib or my family. While I was looking, a man from Gorazde approached my father-in-law.

"Are you from Visegrad?" he said. "My name is Kemo. You're going to stay with me."

"My name is Sead," said my father-in-law. "Thank you for your generous offer, but we have a lot of people with us. We're four families."

"It doesn't matter," said Kemo. "You can all come. I have a big house and it's especially empty right now. My wife and child are away."

My father-in-law finally accepted the invitation and Kemo led our little convoy to his house. He was right, it was big. It was an absolutely beautiful house.

Kemo's two sisters were waiting for us with food. After introductions, we all had lunch together.

"You'll want to rest, of course," said our host's sister. "If I can do anything for you, just call on me. I live right next door." Then the sisters left.

Our host himself told us that if we lacked clothes we were free to look for something in the closets. "We have plenty of food. Help yourselves. And if you need something that you don't see, just go to the grocery store downstairs. Tell the shopkeeper who you are and he'll give it to you."

We didn't need anything other than a place to sleep but were grateful for the man's generosity.

"Thank you," said my father-in-law, a little embarrassed. "We wish we weren't in this situation. One day I hope to return your hospitality under our own roof."

But that would not be for some time. Our apartment was half under water.

"Don't worry about that," said Kemo. "Don't worry about

anything. Stay here as long as you like. I have things to do but the house is open. Come and go as you please."

We finally got some rest and took showers. We felt safe and secure for the first time in days. But we didn't stay put for long. Soon after our host left, we went out to look for my family.

We found them the way you would expect, looking for familiar faces, asking for clues. One boy told us that they were living near the marketplace. We went there. It was a girl I knew, Amela, who finally said, "Yes, I know where your family is. Come on. I'll take you to them."

My brothers, Almir and Samir, were playing in the yard in front of the house. I ran to them and hugged them.

"Jasmina! Suljo! When did you get here?" Then they called up to the house, "Mama! Mama! Jasmina and Suljo are here!" My mother appeared in the doorway and with her came all of my father's extended family—my uncles, aunts, and cousins. We were all together again and we hugged and kissed and cried.

I looked around for my father and Tajib. Rukija, my sister-in-law, was there but not Tajib.

"Tajib is still in Dobrun," said my mother. "And your father went back to Visegrad."

"To Visegrad?" I was shocked. "Why?"

"I couldn't stop him. He said he hadn't hurt anyone, so no one would hurt him. We couldn't convince him to stay."

"He's like a baby, he is so naive!" I was angry at my father and worried about him.

"Why is Tajib still in Dobrun?" Suljo asked. I could see the worry in his face. Suljo didn't have any brothers of his own but he and Tajib were as close as brothers.

My mother didn't have an answer.

There were more reunions that day. When we returned to Kemo's house, it was empty. The other cars were gone and when

Kemo came home he told us that the others had found some cousins in town. "They all wanted to be together. I'm bringing another family from Visegrad to stay. They're related to a good friend of mine. In fact, they're at my sister's house right now."

We didn't ask him who they were so imagine my surprise when Kemo came back with Sabina and her family. Sabina and I screamed and laughed like schoolgirls when we saw each other. "Selma and Dijana are with their families a block from here," Sabina said. "Let's go surprise them!"

When we rang the bell and Selma answered the door, her expression made us break out laughing. She screamed like Sabina and I had screamed and she hollered, "Dijana, come downstairs! Wait till you see who's here!"

We hugged and kissed. To celebrate finding each other, we decided to go to a café.

Gorazde was so full of people I knew and the sounds in the cafés were such happy and familiar sounds, I almost forgot about the war. At last, when I saw a reminder of the fighting, it was the happiest reminder I could have seen.

In one of the cafés, sitting at a table with the men who'd been with him at Dobrun, was Tajib. They were all unshaven and grimy and they were the most beautiful things I'd seen all day. "Where have you been?" I cried and I almost knocked Tajib out of his chair as I rushed to hug him.

Embracing my brother, I felt like I was flying. He stood up to hug me back and I squeezed him as hard as I could. I couldn't pull away from him. The war could have everything if it would only let me keep the people I loved. "Where have you been?" I said again.

"We just arrived," he said. "We were the last ones out of Visegrad. Look at me. I don't have anything to wear. I was going to go back home for some clothes but there wasn't time."

He really was filthy. They all were. They had been living in the woods for days on end.

"I'm so relieved you're all right. It must have been hard in Dobrun."

"There is no Dobrun. Not any more. Even when it was nothing but ruins, the shells kept falling. A lot of people who were just trying to get out were killed by the Serb artillery."

"And Visegrad? Was anyone killed?"

"You know Almir's sister, the one who was pregnant? A shell fell very close and the shrapnel tore her and the baby to bits. Also, a professor from the high school died. Those are the ones I know about."

I had promised myself that I was through with tears but I cried for Almir's sister.

"I don't think they'll be satisfied with just Visegrad and Foca," Tajib said. "A lot of people are getting out of Gorazde and if you ask me, that's smart."

Tajib told Sabina that her house and her uncle's house had been burned down by the Serbs. She already knew. She and her family might never be able to return to Visegrad or even leave Gorazde. The Serbs had a vendetta against anyone with the Sabanovic name after what her Uncle Murat had done with the hydroelectric station. They wouldn't get past the first checkpoint.

Sabina and her family might not have been welcome in Visegrad but the next morning, the Serbs tried to convince the rest of us that we should return. Serbs from Visegrad came to Gorazde with a proclamation. It said that all the Muslims who had fled were free to come home. They guaranteed the safety of all residents, except for those guilty of crimes. Criminals, in their view, included anyone who had tried to defend civilians who were under attack.

The Serbs said they would open the schools, factories, stores and cafés. Everything would go back to normal. But the property of anyone who hadn't returned within two weeks would be confiscated. To make things easy for the refugees, the Serbs supplied Red Cross buses to bring the people back home.

My family decided that they should return.

"Mama, this is crazy!" I told her. "How can you trust them?"

Suljo argued with her, too. "Look at what they've already done!" he said. "Mama, you can't go back. Things are only going to get worse."

But she wouldn't listen to us. "Nurko is already there," she said. "Jasmina, how can I stay here when your father needs me at home? I don't belong here. Look at all the people getting ready to return. If they're all going, why should we stay?" Then my aunt appealed to my mother-in-law. "Mevla, come back with us. Nobody will even touch you. You can all stay with us for as long as you like."

"No," Suljo insisted. "Absolutely not."

"I want to go back," Suljo's mother admitted. "Visegrad is my home. Yesterday, I was on the phone with Persa and she asked when I was coming back."

"And did Persa warn you about the war?" Suljo asked his mother. "She left her house without a word to you. She had an idea what was coming but did she breathe a hint of it to you? Do you think she cares about you?"

"Persa is my best friend," my mother-in-law said.

We couldn't convince my family so we went to the Sports Center to see them off. Even Tajib's pregnant wife returned to Visegrad.

"You see, Suljo?" my mother-in-law persisted. "Everyone is going back."

"If you go, Mama," Suljo said, "you'll have to go alone.

Father, Jasmina and I are going to Sarajevo." I'd never seen Suljo be so cross with his mother.

"I don't want to go back without you," she told him.

"Then let's stop talking about it," Suljo said more gently.

17

Road to Sarajevo

We left Gorazde by car. We had to pass Serbian checkpoints all along the way. The first one was at Ustipraca, a big village at a crossroads between Gorazde and Visegrad.

The units at Ustipraca were Yugoslav Army. When we drove up to the barricade we found ourselves in the midst of about forty soldiers. Three soldiers approached each car as it stopped. One of them started searching our car before any of them had said a word to us.

"Let me see identification for each of you," said one of them.

Another said, "What do you have in the car?"

The man doing the searching looked like he was about twenty. The men were clean-shaven with short hair. I relaxed a little because they were regular soldiers, not Chetniks.

"We have only some clothes and a few blankets. The Drina flooded our house."

"Nothing," said the man who had searched.

"Okay." The first soldier returned our driver's licenses. "You can go."

From there, the road was deserted. There was no traffic in either direction. It was eerie. By the time we were a few kilometers out of Ustipraca, it felt as if we were the last people on earth.

The next checkpoint wasn't like the first. It was a barricade set up outside of Rogatica. The men who guarded it had long beards down to their stomachs and very long hair. I had never seen Serbs like that before. Their clothes were dirty and they bristled with weapons—automatic guns at the ready, knives and hand grenades on their belts.

They were Chetniks of a sort that I had only heard about until then. The long hair and beards were their trademark. It must have taken a long time to grow such a beard. The extremists hadn't sprung up overnight, I realized.

My father-in-law rolled down the window of the car. "Where are you trying to go?" said the man at the barricade. His voice was harsh.

"We're going to Sarajevo," my father-in-law said.

Suljo, my mother-in-law and I sat in silence, not moving. I was worried for Suljo. He was young and strong and the Serbs might not let him into Sarajevo in case he decided to fight.

"Why are you going to Sarajevo?"

"The Drina took our house in Visegrad. We have cousins in Sarajevo. We're going to stay with them."

"Do you have any weapons in the car?"

"No, just clothes and blankets. You can see for yourself if you like."

"Get out."

The checkpoint guard opened the trunk. He and the two Chetniks with him took everything out and searched it while the men in the woods pointed their weapons at us. Then the three men searched the car, under the seats. They found nothing of interest.

The first man looked at me. "Are they your family?" he asked Suljo's father. "Who is she?"

"She is my daughter," said my father-in-law in a rush. I didn't understand why he said that until I considered that Azem had fought in Croatia and Tajib had defended Dobrun and Visegrad. He wanted to keep me from having to answer questions about my family.

The Chetnik kept looking me over, then finally said, "Okay, go!"

As we drove away, I was grateful that the checkpoint guard hadn't been a little more observant. My in-laws had clear blue eyes like Suljo's but mine were brown. We might have had more explaining to do and as soon as we had aroused suspicions, the Chetniks would have been convinced we had something to hide.

Rogatica was in Serbian hands. Chetniks patrolled the streets and there were very few civilians to be seen. The traffic was mostly military. We saw tanks on flatbed trucks.

Suljo's father had the address of a family who, we'd been told in Gorazde, would help us. But their house was empty. They, too, were refugees.

Then we had a stroke of luck. We saw Buba.

"Buba!" said Suljo's father. "Hey, what are you doing here?"

Buba was a policeman and our neighbor in Visegrad. "I'm getting out of here, that's what," he said. "I have a lot of cousins who live here and I've been trying to convince them to get the hell out. When did you get here?"

"Just half an hour ago. We're trying to get to Sarajevo but we don't know what route to take. What's safest?"

"You don't want to go by car from here. I mean, you can

try, but it's much better to travel as part of a large group. There are buses leaving tomorrow morning. You'll have to sleep here overnight. You can stay with one of my cousins. I'll take you there in a little while. First, let's go to a hotel for some coffee, okay?"

We followed Buba to the hotel. Actually, he was taking us to meet someone but he hadn't wanted to say so on the street. "Tajib!" I cried out. "How did you get here? When did you arrive?"

"Keep your voice down, Mince," said my brother in a low voice, smiling. "The walls have ears, okay?"

The friends that I'd also seen at the Gorazde café were with him.

"How'd we get here?" Tajib said, still in a low voice. "Money buys everything."

"You bribed the Chetniks? I don't believe it!"

"Not the Chetniks," said my brother. "We didn't have our passports and we couldn't get out of Gorazde without ID. We paid a taxi driver, a Serb from Gorazde, to go to Visegrad, find Mukadesa and get our passports from her. She got our documents together and gave them to the guy who then drove us from Gorazde to Rogatica. The Serbs didn't pay much attention to the cab because the driver was a Serb. He did all of that for fifteen Deutsche Marks."

They were smart. They might have figured out the only way for them to get out of Gorazde.

"We're going to Sarajevo with the buses tomorrow."

"We're going, too," I told him. It was great news. We'd get to Sarajevo together. Things were finally looking up.

"Where are you staying?" he asked us. When we told him, Tajib said, "If we all have places to sleep then I think we should leave the hotel now. The neighborhood is crawling with more Chetniks by the minute and it would be best to avoid them."

"See you in the morning," we told him, "God willing."

That night lasted forever. We could hear the explosions of shells and grenades in the Muslim villages around the city.

Morning finally came and at the bus stop it appeared that everyone agreed with us that Sarajevo was the place to go. Hundreds were waiting to board the buses.

At last, the buses moved out. I was on one with my in-laws and Tajib was in another. The caravan didn't travel the usual highways but took us on back roads through the woods instead. The ride was bumpy and uncomfortable and I held Suljo's hand until we came to the first checkpoint. The buses stopped in front of an army barracks that was flying the Serbian flag. Tanks and trucks were lined up near the road.

A soldier stood in the doorway of the bus. "Every man off the bus! Now!"

Other soldiers got on the bus and started checking our passports and bags. Other soldiers were going down the ranks of male passengers. I strained to hear the questions and answers.

"Why are you going to Sarajevo? You want to be Alija's soldier, don't you?"

"No, we're escaping the war," said a man. "We're getting out."

"Tell the truth!"

"It's true. I'm just trying to get my wife and child to safety."

It took the Serbs an hour to check all of us. Still, they made us wait. The men weren't initially allowed to return to the bus. At last, the Serbs let us go. I can't adequately describe the wave of relief that washed over me when I saw the men getting back on the bus and reclaiming their seats.

Sarajevo, I was thinking. In Sarajevo we'll be safe.

18

Sarajevo

April 20th, 1992

We only had to stand at the bus stop in Sarajevo for five minutes while waiting for a taxi to know that our assumptions about Sarajevo were sadly naive. We could hear artillery firing in the distance. Shells weren't falling in this part of the city at the moment but buildings nearby had already been destroyed. The streets were nearly deserted. Few taxis came by and when one did, the driver refused to take us to Suljo's grandmother in Buca Potok.

"Are you kidding? That's right underneath Zuc Hill. That's where the big Serb guns are."

"Look, we can hardly walk that distance!"

"Tell you what. I'll drive you to the bottom of the hill and you can walk the rest of the way to Buca Potok."

So that's what we did. Suljo, his parents and I left for Buca Potok. Tajib and his friends stayed behind to look for Azem, who was waiting for them somewhere in the city.

The driver's caution seemed a little overdone when we got to Buca Potok. People were outside in their yards and there was no sign that any shells had fallen there. Suljo's whole extended family greeted us at his grandmother's house. His grandmother was delirious with joy.

When we had greeted everyone, Suljo took me aside. "Look."

Two Serbian flags were flying high on Zuc Hill. The Yugoslav Army was there with rank after rank of tanks and field artillery. Now I understood the taxi driver's fear. It was the residents of Buca Potok who seemed unrealistic.

"Aren't you afraid?" I asked one of Suljo's neighbors. "Well, they're up there, more of them every day. But they haven't fired a single shot at us." Then he added, "We're taking precautions. People stand guard at night at the bottom of the hill, just in case some Chetniks try to get into the village." That made me feel a little better, but not much. From Buca Potok, you could see shells falling into Sarajevo, raising clouds of dust and destruction. As I learned that night, the hail of explosive shells fell on Sarajevo at all hours. I worried about Azem and Tajib, somewhere in the heart of that mess.

I don't think the Bosnians had even one tank under their control yet. Our defense had always been our national army, only it wasn't our army any longer. The civilian population was defenseless against the artillery that fired down from the hillsides. It seemed silly to even think of this as a war. In a war, you have two armies fighting each other. This was more like a shooting gallery. We were little tin ducks for the Serb gunners.

Still, we settled in at Buca Potok and tried to live life as best we could. Suljo and his father took their turns standing guard. The defenders below Zuc Hill had roughly a dozen rifles between them.

We played cards a lot and it was hard not to be lulled into a false sense of security by the lack of any firing directed against us. All day long, the distant rumble of explosions echoed from Sarajevo but Buca Potok remained peaceful.

Tajib, Bahe and Emir frequently made their way through the shelling to come see us. Every time, they brought cigarettes for my in-laws.

"What about Azem?" I asked Tajib. "I haven't seen him for months. Why doesn't he ever come with you?"

"Mince, he sends his love. He's a commandant in the Bosnian Army, now. He's got a million things to think about and he can't go around on social visits, not even to his sister."

I understood but it was hard not seeing him.

"Tell me about the phone call from Mama," Tajib said. She had called the day before, worried about Tajib and Azem. I told him that. I also told him that she'd said things were back to normal, that the children were all going to school again and our father had gone back to work. The Army had tanks on every corner but they seemed to be keeping their word.

"She said Visegrad was much safer than Sarajevo these days. Some houses had been burned down while they were gone but everything's quiet now. But she also made it clear that she couldn't say everything in case the phone was tapped."

"Visegrad won't be safe much longer," Bahe predicted. His family had come from Gorazde to Sarajevo. "I wish your families would get out of there. You know the buses we came here on? Yesterday, when the Chetniks ordered the men off, they never let them get back on. The women and children continued alone. Nobody knows what's become of the men but I think the Serbs just killed them."

Tajib looked depressed as Bahe said this.

"Well," said Emir, whose family had also gone back to Visegrad, "I'd like to know where you think it's safe. Sarajevo?"

"Snipers are getting really bad in the city," Tajib said. "I thought for certain we were going to get shot on the way here today. I don't know how often we're going to be able to do this."

My heart skipped a beat. "Don't! Don't risk yourselves just to visit us!"

"We'll see, Jasmina. The situation's always changing. We'll come when it's safe."

And then they didn't come for days.

The next time I saw them was when I was visiting a neighbor's house with Suljo's mother and grandmother. Suljo's cousin, who was just a child, came to get me.

"Jasmina, come home! Your brothers and their friends are there. Your brother is wounded."

"What? Semir, who? Who is wounded?"

"I don't know which one is which. I just know that one of them is wounded. They carried him into the house."

I ran back to the house as fast as I could. Tajib, Bahe and Emir were there. Azem was with them. His leg and foot were wrapped with bandages and I started to cry. As I hugged and kissed him, Azem said, "Hey, it's okay, Jasmina. I'm fine. It's almost healed."

"This is why you couldn't come see me, isn't it?"

"If Tajib told you I was in the hospital, you'd have thought it was something serious. Now stop crying." His eyes were filling with tears. "Come on, cut it out. You're making me cry. I can't remember when I cried last."

I hugged him again and tried to stop crying. But I couldn't. Soon we were all in tears and it wasn't just because Azem had been wounded. We cried for everything that had happened so far and for what might happen next.

"What happened to you?"

Azem told me that he'd been in a firefight with his men

outside of Sarajevo. The Serbs called in artillery fire and shrapnel hit Azem. "It's mostly healed," he said. "I lost a toe. That's nothing in this war. God saved me when others around me had it much worse." Then he asked, "Have you heard from Mama?"

"She called this morning. The Chetniks are starting to round people up and put them in jail. Six Chetniks with stockings on their heads showed up at the apartment last night looking for Ibrahim. The children were frightened and Mama is afraid to be there now. Our father thinks maybe it was a mistake to come back, after all."

"What else did she say?"

"Bahe, I'm sorry," I said to my brothers' friend. "The Serbs trashed your apartment and looted it. Mukadesa wanted to go and see if anything could be salvaged for you but Tanja was in front of the building keeping a lookout. She tells the Chetniks about anyone who takes an interest in your affairs. My family couldn't even spend much time looking at your apartment from our balcony because Tanja was watching them."

"They should get out," Azem said.

"If they can," Tajib added. "What else did she say?"

"That's about it. I could tell she was afraid to say more." As I related this, I couldn't understand Tanja's behavior.

She hated us now as well as every other Muslim family in Visegrad. My mother said that Tanja turned her head away and wouldn't recognize my family on the street. She was a Chetnik, I guessed. I would never have imagined that she could come to hate Ibrahim and Bahe. She didn't have older brothers and her father drank a lot, so Ibrahim and Bahe had sort of made her their honorary kid sister. Whenever she needed help, they had been there for her.

People could change so fast.

19

"If it's loud, get down fast!"

May 1992

The next morning, Suljo and I were playing cards with some of his grandmother's neighbors. We were having fun and almost able to forget the war for a moment. But the war didn't forget us. We heard a sound—a roar like jets going right over our heads—and then the house shook. The next thing I knew, Suljo was pushing me to the floor and covering me with his body. I heard my mother-in-law's voice. She was screaming.

"Is anyone wounded?" Suljo said, getting up. "Mama, what's wrong?"

She had been in the hallway when the explosion rocked the house. The force of the blast had knocked her back into the room, but she was all right.

"Jasmina, didn't you hear it coming?" Suljo asked.

"I heard something, but I didn't know what it was."

"You've got to react to sounds. If it's loud, get down fast!" Then he squeezed my hand.

Suljo's grandmother had gone outside to inspect the damage. When we heard her scream, we thought something had happened to her and we rushed out.

"My God! Oh, my God!" she wailed.

She was fine, but she was pulling out her hair hysterically. We followed her gaze to the second floor balcony where the shell or the rocket or whatever it was had come down. The balcony was destroyed and there were two bodies in the wreckage. The two men who shared that part of the house were soldiers of the Bosnian Army, though they didn't wear uniforms. They had been able to see the Yugoslav Army positions on Zuc Hill from the balcony and their job was to report any change in activity up there.

Suljo urged his grandmother back into the house then went to the balcony himself to help take the bodies of the dead men to their families' homes.

Since the balcony had a perfectly clear line of sight to the hill, the Yugoslav Army also had a clear view of the balcony. The Serbs had known exactly what they were aiming at.

There were more explosions in Buca Potok. Suljo returned and we decided that we should leave the house. It had taken too much damage. Another shell nearby would collapse it onto us. At first, we huddled with some neighbors but they didn't have a cellar so we found another house that did. A lot of other people had already taken shelter there but we squeezed in with them.

If the Chetniks had happened to come looking for us then, we feared, they could have slaughtered us all in just a few places. There weren't many cellars in Buca Potok.

Suljo, my father-in-law and some other men took the rifles and went to stand guard at the bottom of the hill. Those of us left behind in the cellar could hardly move. There were forty of us but no one dared to leave. Shells fell faster and faster, more than one a second. The ground never stopped shaking.

Someone had a radio. We could hear only bits and snatches between explosions but it kept us occupied, listening to the reports of which parts of Sarajevo were taking the heaviest shelling. The announcer read a list of buildings that had been destroyed and gave a count of Bosnians killed in the city so far. The radio was a comfort, though I'm not sure why war news comforted us in the midst of a barrage.

We couldn't even leave the cellar to go to the bathroom. The children cried but there wasn't any place to put them to sleep so their mothers held them in their laps.

I hoped that Suljo and his father were all right. I worried about Azem, Tajib and the others. Was the attack just as bad everywhere? Or was Buca Potok getting the worst of it?

We stayed in that cramped little hole for the better part of two days without food. It was night when they finally let up and Suljo came to see us. He assured me that all the men who had stood guard were fine.

"But every house in Buca Potok is destroyed," he said. "I think the shelling has stopped because they just don't have much to shoot at any more."

Suljo's grandmother left the cellar and went to what was left of her kitchen to see if she could cook something up to help feed everyone.

"Jasmina, do you want to get out of here for a while?" asked Suljo. "We'll help my grandmother make bread."

"Sure."

I was afraid that the Serbs would start shooting again at any moment but I'd had enough of the cellar.

I couldn't believe the devastation that greeted me after those two days of shelling. Roofs were generally gone and quite a few walls had been knocked down, too. Suljo named some of the dead that he knew about and I noticed that the news didn't affect me much. The first dead bodies I had seen had devastated me but now my grieving started and finished within the span of a heartbeat. Death was too common to slow down for. Depression and sorrow could only get in the way of staying alert and thinking about how to survive.

We returned to the cellar with the food from Suljo's grandmother and found a vigorous discussion in progress. Everyone was trying to imagine what part of Sarajevo might be safe. Almost everyone agreed that they had to leave Buca Potok but there was still the question of what place would be safer.

Suljo and I decided that we should see Azem and Tajib about finding a place to stay in Sarajevo. On the way down the hill with Suljo and my in-laws, we met a man, Suad, who was in the Bosnian Army. He'd been in Sarajevo earlier that day.

"Suad, do you know my brothers, Tajib and Azem? Do you know where I can find them?"

"Of course I know Azem. My superior officer reports to him. Your brother is an important man."

It was nice to hear of my brother's importance but what I really wanted to know was if he was still alive and, if so, where.

"I just came up to check on my wife and child," Suad said. "I'm moving them to a hotel in Sarajevo. Everyone up here is going to have to move." Since he was headed back to Sarajevo, he promised to get a message to Azem or Tajib.

We went back to wait and Tajib eventually came to get us. "I'm so glad to see you," I told him. "Buca Potok was terrible."

"I heard on the radio. I thought about you but unfortunately Sarajevo wasn't faring any better. I think we should hurry now. Azem told me to bring you right back."

"Tajib," said my mother-in-law, "do you have a cigarette?" She had run out of cigarettes before the artillery attack.

"Ah, Mevla, I forgot to bring you some. Here, take mine."

"You've saved me again, Tajib." She fumbled to light one. "I'd die without cigarettes." Then she started to cry. "Now watch out for my Suljo. I'm not happy that these two are leaving me but they want to be with you and Azem. Maybe they'll be safer."

"Please don't cry," I told her. "We'll come to see you as often as we can. We'll bring you cigarettes."

Suljo hugged her. "Mama, take care."

"You too my son. Be careful."

It was on the way back to Sarajevo that Suljo said to Tajib that it seemed a shame to waste the military training he'd had in the Yugoslav Army. I knew where the conversation was headed and I knew that I couldn't stop it. It would have been selfish of me to try. I wanted Suljo beside me to always protect me but he would want to protect other people in our young country as well.

"Exactly how does one enlist in the Bosnian Army?" he asked.

20

City Under Siege

Summer 1992

Downtown Sarajevo was like the end of the world. There was rubble everywhere in the streets and some people were living in the barest remains of buildings.

Our new home was the Belgrade Hotel in the heart of Sarajevo's older district. The Belgrade, with its popular disco in the basement, had been a nice hotel before the war that appealed especially to young people. The disco, of course, was long gone. From the early days of the siege, every basement in Sarajevo had been converted into a bomb shelter.

In fact, basements were Sarajevo real estate. Property values change in a city ringed by hostile artillery. A house missing one wall and a chunk of its roof could still command a high price if it had a good, solid cellar. On the other hand, if an unscathed beautiful house packed with luxuries didn't have a basement, forget it.

With a good basement, you might even try to attract an

international personality. There weren't many politicians who would travel to Sarajevo those days and most who did come usually touched down for a photo opportunity and then high-tailed it. The few who lingered, though, either stayed at the Holiday Inn with the journalists or sought out someone with a strong basement.

The Belgrade Hotel was now a barracks for the Bosnian fighters and their families. Azem commanded this sector of the city, though those around him did not call him Azem any longer. His nom de guerre was Zenga. Most of the important officers were from Sarajevo and didn't have to adopt aliases but Azem did so to protect our family members who were in Serb-controlled areas of the country.

In the Zagreb Hotel, three blocks away, were Tajib and our other friends. The Zagreb was an army barracks, too, though all of these places harbored refugees as well. Space was scarce and the Bosnian Army was, in any case, an improvised one. Few of the soldiers wore uniforms. Azem did, but he was a commander. Most of our defenders went to the front lines in street clothes.

We lived most of the time without water or electricity. Things that broke, whatever they were, generally stayed broken—there were no spare parts. There wasn't much to eat except for U.N. relief supplies and those were mostly rice.

There wasn't a lot of economic activity during the siege. People had quite a bit of time on their hands and they spent much of it thinking about things to eat. The women of Sarajevo were inventive cooks. They made a sort of cheese substitute from rice by cooking it for a long time in soup. Then they'd spread the resulting paste between thin layers of dough. People foraged, too. They learned to create casseroles from backyard garden snails and they made pies from cooked nettles. With water scarce, though, even creative cooks found it hard at times to turn their meager resources into something edible.

I had no contact with my family in Visegrad in those days. The Chetniks had destroyed the post office at Gorazde that was a key link for phone lines. We had very little contact with the outside world at all. There was a radio operator in our building who, when there was electricity, sometimes got messages in and out as well as received broadcast news. That's how we heard about the rape camps that the Serbs maintained.

Our life in the hotel was communal. We were like a big family sharing the tasks of acquiring and preparing food. All the men and some of the women went out to fight every day or for a few days at a time.

My best friend in those days was Suada, an unmarried woman of thirty-eight who lived in the hotel with her parents. On one of the rare days when we had electricity, I was watching television when I heard her shout as she came into my room, "Jasmina! We have water, too!"

Water was always great news. Suada and I could wash the dishes. Better still, no one would have to stand in the long lines of people waiting for water outside. Such lines were always hazardous as they often drew shelling from the Serbs. Anywhere we gathered, they tried to kill many of us at once. While waiting for water, waiting for bread or waiting for rice, you risked your life.

A bread line had been hit a few days earlier. Shrapnel had claimed fifty lives and wounded many more Bosnians. Then the Serbs kept up the shelling and the sniper fire, trying to kill the people who worked to take the wounded to the hospital. All this happened just outside our hotel, painting the street with blood. Suljo and Suada and I were lucky. We had been walking that street just an hour before.

"Water," I said to Suada, who now stood in my room. "That's very good news." But I didn't smile.

"Jasmina, what's wrong? First electricity and now water!" But the electricity was part of why I was sad. I almost wished I hadn't been able to watch the television.

"There was a report about Visegrad," I told Suada. Serbs had filled the mosques with people and then set them on fire. "We should never have let my mother go back to Visegrad. But she wouldn't listen!"

"I'm so sorry, Jasmina," Suada said. "Try not to think about it. You have to be strong. And what's the difference, really, between Sarajevo and Visegrad? We're dying every day all over the country. But some of us will live. Be strong, okay?" She was right. I could die at any moment, as could Suljo, Tajib or Azem. But it was different to die because a shell exploded next to you or because a distant sniper picked you out. I was much more afraid of the kind of killing that was happening in Visegrad. It was face-to-face murder. Whole families were burned alive.

I was afraid for my little sister, afraid that she would be raped.

Even Suljo's return from the fighting that evening did little to console me. I listened to the news but there was only a repetition of the same horrible reports. When we went to bed, I lay awake next to my husband for the longest time, trying not to cry and then giving in to tears.

"Why wouldn't they listen?" Suljo said. "They should never have gone back."

I thought he had been sleeping. He put his arm around me.

"Oh, Suljo. I love you so much. I pray that God keeps you safe. I couldn't live without you."

"Don't worry about me," he said. "I'll be fine. We'll be fine."

Knowing that he was next to me was a comfort. He wrapped

both arms around me and I snuggled into the safety of his warm chest.

At that time, Suljo was assigned to duty outside of the Marshal Tito barracks of the Yugoslav Army. That's where he reported again the next morning.

The barracks, a large military base, really, was right in the middle of Sarajevo. Being anywhere near the barracks was dangerous because the Yugoslav Army was still inside and snipers shot from there. No one who strayed into the line of fire was safe, whether man, woman or child. From the barracks, the Yugoslav Army could also shoot into the Muslim villages outside of the city or direct the fire of other Serb units.

The Bosnian Army understandably made the expulsion of these troops a high priority and they wanted to accomplish it without a massive battle. Azem was one of the key negotiators and he was the only Bosnian who was allowed to enter the barracks to talk to the Serb commandant.

In this one case, Bosnians had some leverage against the Serbs. Sarajevo surrounded the barracks just as the Serbs surrounded Sarajevo. There was a siege going on within the siege.

At last, the Serbs capitulated. They were granted safe passage out of the city but they would have to leave some of their supplies behind. The uniforms, food and even weapons that they couldn't take with them became a windfall for the Bosnian defenders of the city.

I first heard of the Yugoslav Army pull-out on the radio. The supreme commander of the Bosnian Army, Sefer Halilovac, thanked the three commanders who had negotiated on the Bosnian side. He thanked them by name and for a moment I was very proud at hearing that Azem Dervisevic had played a key role.

Then my heart froze with fear. Why hadn't Halilovic expressed his gratitude to "Zenga" instead? Now the Serbs knew the names of three high-ranking officers in the defense of Sarajevo. What if the Serbs in Visegrad decided to take revenge on my family?

In spite of my renewed fear for my family, this was a day for celebration in Sarajevo. Snipers in the barracks had killed a lot of people and that would finally stop.

That night, Tajib and our friends from the Hotel Zagreb came to celebrate with us.

"I'm so proud of you!" I told Azem when he arrived.

He smiled broadly. "We worked a long time on that and it finally worked."

"Did you hear that Sefer read your real name on the radio?"

"I heard. I don't know why he did that. Maybe the news won't travel, if we're lucky." Like all of us, he was eager to put bad thoughts aside. This day was a victory and it had been accomplished without a casualty on either side.

As I stood talking to Azem, I noticed that he kept looking at one part of the room. I followed his gaze just as he said, "Look at that woman. She's beautiful. Do you know who she is?"

I recognized her, though I had never talked to her. She was Ana Katarina Petrovic, a photojournalist from America. She was tall with deep, dark eyes and black hair. She was the sort of woman who was effortlessly beautiful. We often saw her around the hotel's children—they liked her a lot.

Azem finally got up the courage to ask her to join us. Here he was, the hero of the day, but he was still a little shy around a beautiful woman.

When she joined us, we were all charmed by her accent. She had a great vocabulary in Serbo-Croatian though her grammar was not as strong. Still, we could understand everything she said and she seemed to understand us.

"We don't hear many foreigners speaking our language," Suljo observed.

"I'm of Yugoslav heritage," she explained. "My father is a Serb from Belgrade and my mother is Slovenian. They live in America now, though. That's where I was born."

It didn't bother us that her father was a Serb—she was obviously there to help us by telling our story to the world. It's worth saying again that not all Serbs were our enemies. There were Serbs in the Bosnian Army, and the national government of Bosnia was still made up of a mixture of Serbs, Muslims and Croats.

From that night on, Katarina was our friend. We spent a lot of hours together talking about our lives before the war and our hopes for the future. We talked about ordinary things, too, like food and water, the daily topics for people under siege.

One night, Katarina came to our room. "Jasmina, tell me about your brother. I want to know all about him. Is he a good person?"

Azem must have asked her out. Clearly she was interested, but apprehensive. As a woman, I could understand her caution, especially in the middle of a war in a foreign land. But how could I reassure her about Azem? I loved him. He was my brother and a wonderful man. What more could I say?

Suljo said, "It's no good to ask Jasmina about Azem. He's her brother, so of course she won't say anything bad. Ask me and I'll tell you the truth." He was grinning.

"Suljo!"

He made a helpless gesture, still smiling.

"Suljo is right, Katarina. I think the world of Azem, but I'm not the one to ask. I can tell you, though, that you are exactly his type."

A few days later, they started going out. Before too long, they had moved into the same room of the hotel. It was clear that they were very happy together. Very swiftly, they had fallen deep in love.

Katarina & Azem

Love could develop quickly in the midst of war. Friendship, too. During the day, Katarina would often stay with me while the men went off to fight. One day, she said, "Jasmina, you're like a sister to me. Please accept this ring. My mother gave it to me for good luck. Now I want to grant good luck to you."

It was a beautiful gold ring with a diamond setting. But I said, "I can't accept a gift that came from your mother."

Katarina insisted. I finally relented and she put the ring on my left hand since my wedding ring was on my right.

"I love it," I told her. "Thank you, Katarina."

Those were hellish days, with the war going on day-after-day like a bad dream from which we could never wake up. And all the while, we met new people and made fast friends. People fell in love and celebrated every day. And every day, people died violent deaths.

Some days, you regretted that you loved anyone because it tore your heart when someone close to you died. Other days, you were grateful for your friends above all else because the unbearable, shared, could be borne.

Evenings, Suljo and I played cards with friends, trying to make a party of every gathering. Then, when he went off to fight, I sat listening to all of the explosions and rifle reports, wondering where he was and praying to God to protect him. Each time, I imagined him coming back to me safe and whole. But I couldn't help imagining that he might come back wounded or not at all.

The occasional successes of the Bosnian Army were a double-edged sword. When our army took a little bit of territory, the shelling of civilian targets increased.

One night, in the midst of a campaign to push the Serbs back, Suada and I almost stayed too long in the line of fire. It was seven p.m. and we were washing dishes after dinner. Suljo was several blocks away in the Hotel Zagreb teaching other soldiers what he had learned in the Yugoslav Army about explosives. It had been his specialty and Azem had told him to teach the essentials to ten soldiers every day. They were going to put a lot of explosive devices around the defensive perimeter of the city in the hopes of discouraging the Serbs from taking back whatever territory the Bosnian Army gained.

As Suada and I did the dishes, the women and children were finishing dinner when some shells came down very close to the hotel. Windows broke and the children started to scream. There was glass everywhere in the kitchen but miraculously, no one had been cut.

"Into the cellar!" shouted one of the mothers.

They all headed for shelter while Suada and I kept washing the dishes. Suddenly, several more shells exploded at once. Suada was terrified.

"Jasmina, we should get to the cellar, too!"

The explosions had shaken me up, also. Still, exploding shells were part of life. Sometimes they fell close, sometimes far away. Ever since Buca Potok, I tried to take the shelling in stride. I just didn't feel like running away and letting the attackers control me. Besides, a shell could penetrate and kill you no matter where you were hiding.

"Don't worry, Suada. We'll be all right." We kept doing dishes.

"Suada, Jasmina!" shouted a soldier from the doorway. "Are you crazy? Stop washing the dishes and go to the cellar right now!"

Suada was visibly relieved. She hadn't wanted to leave me but she certainly didn't want to stay. When we got to the cellar, we found everybody else was already there. Azem and Katarina were talking to some wounded Bosnian soldiers who were lying on the floor. It was cold, so Katarina and I went upstairs to get blankets for them. As we got to the ground floor, Suljo came into the hotel.

"Suljo, thank God you're all right!" Then I scolded him. "Why did you come now? You could have been killed!" Even though I had confidence that I could stay inside the kitchen without harm, I knew better than to venture onto the streets at a time like this. "You should have waited for the shelling to let up."

"I couldn't stay at the Zagreb. I had a bad feeling and I was afraid for you. I ran the whole way. It's hell out there. It feels like the whole city is falling down."

"We're fetching blankets. You can help us. Are Tajib and Bahe all right? Emir and the others?"

"They decided to stay in the Zagreb. There's no basement there. I hope they'll be okay."

The shells fell faster and faster. Together, we rounded up enough blankets. As we went back into the cellar, we could feel a change in the vibration of the explosions. The shells were now landing directly on the hotel.

It wasn't long before the cellar began to fill with smoke. Some of the men went upstairs again. A soldier came back down and told us, "The top two floors of the hotel are on fire! We've got to put it out before it spreads!"

"Stay here!" Suljo told me. The men grabbed the firefighting equipment that was kept in the basement.

Shells kept pounding the area around the hotel so we couldn't evacuate the building. Even worse, the flames motivated the Serb gunners to concentrate their barrage on our building. When they previously hit the Europa Hotel, setting it aflame, Serb snipers found the women and children fleeing from the basement easy targets. There were no soldiers in the Europa. The victims were all refugees.

Suljo left to help fight the fire. Soon, the Bosnian firemen arrived, too. Firemen, doctors and ambulance drivers in Bosnia were such heroes. They showed up even in the heaviest artillery barrages. They made inviting targets but they did their jobs just the same.

It still took quite some time to control the fire. The smoke let up some in the cellar but it wasn't until two in the morning that we were able to breathe smoke-free air again.

Soldiers who had fought the fire made their way to the

basement. I gasped when I saw Suljo. All the men looked bad but he looked worst of all. He was soaking wet and his eyes were blood-red from the smoke. He couldn't see clearly and he was shivering terribly.

"Suljo, are you okay?"

"I'm all right, I'm fine." He explained that he'd been the one closest to the fire, so that's why he looked as roughed up as he did. "We beat it," he said. "The top two floors are gone but we saved the other four."

"Let's go up to the room. You need dry clothes. Look at how you're shaking!"

We went upstairs. Outside, it was quiet. The Serbs had stopped shooting for the time being.

21

—

Rape & Murder: The Tools of Genocide

What we were enduring in Sarajevo was bad enough but we kept hearing reports about the progress of the Serbs' "ethnic cleansing" campaign. Systematic rape was part of the campaign. Some women were raped in their homes and released, some were raped and killed, and some were sent to rape camps where they were raped again and again, day after day. Sometimes little girls were raped to death. Some women were kept in the rape camps until they conceived and were six months along in their pregnancy. Then they were released so that they would "go home and bear little Serbs."

When the Bosnian Army retook a Muslim village that had fallen to the Serbs, they often found bodies in the most hideous places—stuffed into washing machines or dishwashers. People too old or too sick to get out of bed were found still in bed with their throats cut.

It's hard to understand the motives for such atrocities. If all the Serbs wanted was the Bosnians' land, wasn't it enough to drive them out of their homes by force? Why rape? Why torture?

The sad truth, I am afraid, is that there are men who would willingly be criminals in any case. War gives them cover, even encouragement, to do the most horrible things without fear of justice. That was one of the horrors of the siege—knowing that such people were among the soldiers encircling our city and that outside of Sarajevo, awful crimes were being perpetrated, possibly against those whom we loved most…and none of us could help them.

I know it's hard to read about these things. Believe me, it is harder still to live in the country where it's happening, to not have news of your family for weeks on end while such horrors are reported on the radio.

We suffered and we felt a deep despair. The longer the siege ground on, the more dreadful were the reports of atrocities. We felt horribly alone while the world watched us on television. They could see how the Serbs used their heavy weapons to pound away at the civilian populations while trying to starve us. But little was done to help us. Naturally, we were grateful for the food convoys—when they were permitted to get to us. But the longer the U.N. was in Bosnia, the less they did. The few times when there was tough action against the Serbs, the guns around Sarajevo went silent for a while. But tough action was rare.

And what we needed in any case was not direct intervention by NATO. We needed to have the right restored to us to match the big guns of our attackers with big weapons of our own. But the arms embargo against us was kept in place in the interests of keeping the war contained.

It was as if the world had come upon a rape victim while the crime was in progress and tied her hands so that she wouldn't do something violent to the rapist.

Tajib brought me news of a phone call one day. "All the Muslims in Visegrad are being expelled. There's a hotel in central Bosnia where many of them are ending up as refugees. When you call the hotel, they'll give you the names of the people who are there."

My heart was beating wildly. "Tajib, did you call?"

"I did. The man found the names of our Aunt Cimija, and some cousins. I asked if I could please talk to my aunt to ask about other family members, but he couldn't do that. He said he has so many people calling that he can only check the list of names."

I was crushed. I thought he'd have news about our parents. Tajib and I were talking about how else we might get in touch with our aunt when Azem came into the room.

"We called the radio operator in Central Bosnia," he said. "There's no word yet but the people there will get in touch with our radio man if they learn anything about our family. Jasmina, tomorrow Tajib and I will be on the front lines so you'll have to go to the radio room and check for messages yourself."

That night, I couldn't sleep. If I could have, I'd have gone to the radio room and sat with the operator all night so that I was there the moment a message came. But the radio was important for military operations, too, and I'd be in the way.

As I was tossing and turning, I discovered that Suljo was still awake, too. "Do you think they made it to Central Bosnia?" he asked.

I was almost angry with him for asking that. Of course I hoped that they were safe. But so many terrible things could have happened to them.

I reminded myself that Suljo was as worried for them as I was and he wanted to talk about it. "I bet they made it," I said. "I bet they're already safe." But my heart was full of painful doubts.

Suljo and Azem left early the next morning. I made myself eat breakfast and then went to see the radio operator.

"Hey," I said, trying to sound casual. "Got any news for me?"

"Yes. I have a message. Your family arrived in Central Bosnia-"

I cut off the rest of his sentence with a scream of joy. *They were out! They had made it! Just wait until I told Suljo and my brothers! Thank God. Thank God, they were okay.*

"Jasmina," said the operator quietly, "there's more to the message. Your brother Samir wasn't with your family. Neither was your father."

The joy drained away.

"What do you mean? Where are they?"

It was possible that the Serbs hadn't let my father pass some checkpoint. I'd heard that the Serbs were only letting women and children escape, though I'd also hoped that wasn't true. But why would they keep Samir? He was just a kid of fifteen. And if they kept Samir, why not his twin, Almir?

"I don't know, Jasmina. The Serbs might have put Samir in a hotel called Vilina Vlas, in Visegrad."

I knew the Vilina Vlas. That was the hotel with the glassed-in swimming pool. It was where my sister Mukadesa had her salon. The Serbs had taken it over early in the war and turned it into a rape camp. They would not have taken Samir there. The operator was telling me this to hide something from me. Why would he lie, unless...

I saw black spots and I couldn't breathe. I couldn't stand to be in that radio room a moment longer. I ran from there to our room where I was surprised to find that Suljo had returned. He said Azem and Tajib would soon join us.

Looking at Suljo's face, I could see that he knew something terrible.

Azem was shouting when he arrived so I heard him coming down the hallway before I saw him. "How could they?" he shouted. "He was a child!" My Uncle Smail entered the room with Azem and Tajib. Azem kept asking again and again, "How could they do such a thing?" He hit his head against the wall. I'd never seen Azem so crazy with grief.

"Azem, tell me. What happened to Samir?" I was afraid I already knew but I had to hear them speak the words.

"They killed him."

God, please, no. Let them say that the Serbs had done something terrible to Samir but had let him live. Please, please...

Jasmina's brother, Samir

"I'm going to call our mother," Tajib said. "Maybe I can find out more." I grabbed Tajib by the arm. "Wait. Tell me what you already know."

He shook his head. "Not enough. I don't know yet who did it or how." Then he left.

Katarina came into the room and other people started filing in to tell us how sorry they were at the news. I knew that their attention was intended to help us bear Samir's death but I couldn't listen to anyone's words of condolences. I wanted to be alone with Suljo and my brothers. The room was swimming around me.

After an hour, the last of them left. Suljo and I were alone. Suljo pulled at his hair and tears streamed down his face. He shouted himself hoarse.

"Jasmina, I can't believe I'll never see him again."

I comforted him as best I could. Suljo, like his father, had a very tender heart.

I wanted to cry, too, but as I rocked with Suljo, I could feel some cold, dark shadow inside telling me that this was just the start of our grief.

"Suljo," I said. "This war is just beginning. If Samir is the only member of our families to die, then we'll have something to thank God for. I just pray that God keeps you safe." If Samir had died before the war, I'd have been paralyzed with grief. But now I surprised myself. I bitterly felt the loss of my brother yet I wasn't overcome. I could be strong. We had to be strong.

I thought about Samir's dreams of playing professional soccer. I saw the smile on his face when he used to talk about it. Some of the boys he played soccer with had been Serbs. Growing up, we never imagined that some of the boys on his teams would be killed because they had Muslim names while others were spared because they had Serb names.

Why hadn't it been possible for all of us to stand together against these horrors? Why were so many of our old friends collaborators in our destruction?

Tajib was eventually able to tell us the whole story. Getting the truth took some doing because even our mother didn't know that Samir was dead, she thought he was in a concentration camp somewhere. "Almir knows everything," Tajib told us, "but he hasn't been able to bring himself to tell her the story."

Because Samir and Almir were twins, Almir was probably

in more pain than anyone over his brother's death. From the window of my parents' apartment, Almir had seen Samir's abduction.

The man who took him was a Serb named Lukic. He was twenty-three years old and had come from a village right next to Visegrad. For one year, Lukic had gone to high school with my sister, Mukadesa. He lived in Germany for a while but he had to leave that country because of some trouble he'd gotten into—it was never clear to me just what he'd done. He then went to Serbia and trained young men in an extremist paramilitary group. He had returned to Visegrad at the start of the war.

In the first days of the war, Lukic murdered a rich woman in Visegrad and commandeered her car. Later, he killed the woman's husband and son as well while two of their daughters managed to escape from Visegrad.

It was this stolen car that Almir saw turn up our street one day when Samir, a neighbor and a boy who lived with my family were playing in front of our building. That third boy was from Foca. He had fled from the fighting there and my mother met him when the family fled to Gorazde. It was soon clear that his parents had not escaped Foca alive so my family sort of adopted him and brought him back to Visegrad.

By then, everyone knew that it was dangerous to be outside but my mother didn't know that Samir and two other boys had slipped out of the apartment.

Lukic and his accomplices forced the three boys into the car and drove off with them. Almir didn't tell our mother what he had seen even when she grew frantic looking for the three boys. He was worried about his twin, too, but he was sure that there was nothing to be done except to hope and pray. Lukic was outside the law. There would be no one to appeal to for Samir's release. Almir thought it would be worse for my mother to know who had her son. It might even be dangerous for her to try to do anything about it.

Days later, my mother finally tracked down the neighbor boy. He was clearly scared about something but he denied knowing anything about Samir and the other boy.

It was Almir who got the truth out of this neighbor boy when they were alone. The Serbs had threatened to kill the boy if he talked and he was ashamed because of the way he'd saved himself. The Serbs had let him live because he agreed to tell them which of his neighbors had owned guns before the war.

Lukic and his companions took all three boys to a bridge. They threw Samir from the bridge and shot at him on the way down as if for target practice. Then they did the same to the second boy who had escaped from Foca only to be murdered in Visegrad.

I thought then of little Bojan, of the efforts by my brothers to bring his body out of the Drina River for a proper burial. No one would do the same for these two boys. They would stay in the Drina forever, along with so many others.

The Serbs in Visegrad seemed to like this method of execution. My friend, Neza, and his father were shot on the Na Drini Cuprija bridge while Neza's mother and sister watched from their balcony. The bodies were thrown into the river. It was the same for my friend, Manjo.

By the time we were able to speak to our mother in Visoko, she knew the truth. "We were lucky," she said, "to lose only one. We were lucky that Amira wasn't raped."

Visegrad had turned into a nightmare in the last days. People cowered in their houses, afraid to set foot on the streets. But the Serbs came for them where they hid. People were burned alive in their houses or rounded up in the mosques which were then blocked off and set ablaze.

My mother's mother and one of my uncles were burned alive in their house. In World War II, my grandmother had been the only member of her family to escape such a burning. Now, fifty years later, she had not been able to save herself.

The killing went on and on. Perhaps reading this is numbing. Certainly, we were numbed by it. My sister-in-law Rukija's father and two brothers were killed. Our good friend Sule's two brothers were murdered and his sister-in-law was horribly raped. Serbs tied her naked to the hood of a car and drove around with her, stopping now and then to rape and torture her again and again.

To escape such treatment, a beautiful woman named Jasna got out of the rape camp at the Vilina Vlas hotel the only way she could. She jumped from the third floor.

This was Visegrad. This was the city I had grown up in, the place that I loved so much. I had cried whenever I had left it.

And this was our life in Sarajevo: An average of twenty civilians died each day of the siege. Snipers targeted children. There was a Serb slogan about how all "Turkish" women and children must die. The Chetniks not only wanted to drive us from the land, they wanted to wipe us out forever. And all the while, we lived with the news of what was happening elsewhere, in the cities and villages under Serb control.

It was during this time that we received confirmation that my father was being held in a concentration camp. The Serbs tried to orchestrate a trade with Azem but it didn't come to pass. I prayed that they didn't torture my father. I prayed that he would survive.

22

We All Served

Amidst so much pain and chaos, a bright spot was that our Bosnian Army was growing. Our military headquarters were transferred from the hotels to the barracks that the Serbs had evacuated. Azem, Suljo, Tajib and others with experience moved into the barracks and began to divide their time between fighting and teaching the skills of war. The arms blockade kept us at a disadvantage but unlike the Serbs, we were fighting for our lives and for our families. The soldiers trained hard and those who had the expertise improvised weapons from our meager resources.

I wanted to contribute something, too, so I volunteered to work at the Kosevo Hospital. In order to be closer to the hospital, Suljo and I moved again. A friend of my Uncle Smail gave us the use of half of his house for however long we needed it.

The hospital was still a half hour's walk from our new home. That commute was the most dangerous part of my day. On days when the shelling around me grew intense, I had to lie flat on my face in the middle of the street. If you were caught outside, that was the safest thing to do—the shrapnel might miss you and the rubble falling from buildings was less likely to land on you.

Some days, my uncle would say, "Jasmina, don't go to work today. Listen to how the Serbs are shooting! It's too dangerous to go out."

But I would go anyway. All I had to do was think of the wounded in the hospital. They had gone through so much and still had so much more to endure. I couldn't fail them. My job in the administration building was not as urgently vital as that of the doctors and nurses but it was still important. And after I braved the shelling and got to work, I always found that I wasn't alone. Everyone else showed up, too, every single day.

With my boss, Faruk, I kept an inventory of the hospital's food and worked to keep us supplied. Most of our supplies—cooking oil, sugar, flour, or rice—came from the Bosnian Army. They fed wounded civilians as well as their own soldiers. It was hard, anxious work. As soon as we thought we had enough supplies to last a few days, there'd be a flood of wounded to the hospital and we'd end up with nothing to feed them. Five or six hundred patients can go through a lot of food in a short time.

The part of the building where Faruk and I worked also housed the hospital laundry. Often, there wasn't water to wash the soiled or bloody sheets and it smelled horrible. In fact, the entire hospital smelled. There was no air conditioning. Without water to clean with, the smells were often overpowering. The food, for all our efforts, was terrible. I never felt much like eating in the hospital. I kept myself going during the day with coffee. Coffee kept me on my feet no matter what I saw in the clinics.

Everything was in constant motion in the hospital. It was the place that absorbed the crises of Sarajevo. Parts of the city might be quiet at any given time but the hospital never was.

Suljo was hardly ever free. Sometimes he managed to get away long enough to visit me at the hospital but the visits were never longer than ten minutes. Sometimes we didn't see each other for days on end. The war was our life.

Besides rounding up supplies for the hospital, I also brought food, coffee and cigarettes to people who needed them. Lots of people who hadn't smoked before the war had started smoking. A cigarette was a small, predictable pleasure in the midst of chaos.

Every week, I found cigarettes for Suljo's family. They stayed in Sarajevo for a time but had finally been able to move back to Buca Potok when the Bosnian Army took Zuc Hill from the Serbs. That had been our biggest military victory to date and a cause of great celebration. We had astonished even ourselves because it had been a battle of David and Goliath—only Goliath, in that fight, had the sling. Yet we had prevailed.

People in Buca Potok fixed up their houses enough to make them livable. Some factories in the area even started working again.

One of the really amazing things about the siege was the persistence of the press. Television stations, radio stations and newspapers continued their work. The whole building of Oslobodenje, one of the largest newspapers in Bosnia, was bombed down to a crumbling shell. The journalists moved everything they could salvage into the basement and continued to operate from there. Not one issue was canceled. When they ran low on paper, they took to printing just a few copies of each edition and posted them around the city. The paper was never more than a few pages but that it survived at all seemed miraculous.

A lot of journalists—Bosnians and foreigners—died while trying to tell the story of what was happening in Sarajevo.

In these darkest times, it was amazing to see how people helped each other. A girl who lived on the other side of the house from where we lived brought me water every day. She knew that I worked and that Suljo wasn't often home. Water was precious. It was rare and getting it was dangerous. She had to stand in line risking her life for just a few liters but she still shared that water with us.

When I had coffee or if I found some treasure such as candy, I gave it to her and her family. Bosnians had shared before the war. Now we shared more than ever.

23

Searching for Normalcy During War

There were celebrations, even in wartime, as there always had been. Seta and Tajib came by one day to tell me, "Azem and Katarina are getting married tonight. Get ready. We'll pick you up in twenty minutes."

Twenty minutes? How was I supposed to get ready for a wedding in twenty minutes?

"You could have given me some advance notice!" I said. Katarina had told me that she and Azem were planning to get married and had asked me to be a witness. But nobody knew the day and time of the wedding until the last minute. Azem had been afraid that word would get to the Serbs and that they would shell the neighborhood during the ceremony.

I had two liters of water for washing my hair. I managed it, though of course there was no electricity for drying.

Among the clothes I had from Visegrad were the black dress and matching jacket from my graduation party. I never imagined when I bought them that I'd wear that outfit to my brother's wedding.

By the time Tajib returned, I was ready, though still a bit damp.

The wedding was held in Bistrik at the office of the Yugoslav Army's General Kukanjac. The Yugoslav Army had been forced to abandon the building. It was spacious and sturdy, a good place for a wedding.

When we arrived, Azem was already there, wearing a suit. It was the first time since the start of the war that I'd seen him without a uniform. Katarina wasn't there yet. It was a Bosnian tradition for the official witnesses of the wedding to pick up the bride, so Mirza, Rus and I went to the Belgrade Hotel to get her.

Mirza, a married man with two children, was one of Azem's best friends. He had been a bomb expert for the police and now assembled grenades. He was one of the first men to join the Bosnian Army.

Rus, another of Azem's friends, had found a video camera so he came with us to record the event.

We found Katarina waiting for us in a white suit. Her hair was styled very nicely—she looked gorgeous. Mirza gave her a flower and we noticed that her hands were trembling.

"How are you feeling?" I asked her as we escorted her to the car.

"Good," she said. "I just never dreamt that my wedding would be here and in the middle of a war. Azem told me that we were getting married today just two hours ago. I didn't think I'd have time to get ready but we found a hairdresser who would come to the hotel."

"You look great!" I told her.

At Kukanjac's office, Mirza walked in and said, "Azem, I fetched your wife for you. Now don't lose her again!"

Everyone clapped as Azem took Katarina's hand. They looked so elegant together.

Moments later, Suljo and some other soldiers arrived. They were dirty and still had their weapons with them. That was so typical, soldiers coming straight from the fighting to a wedding. That's how things happened. Celebrations never took place without reminders of the war.

"I'm sorry I couldn't go home to change clothes," Suljo told me. "You look beautiful."

"Thank you. I miss you so much. I hardly ever see you any more."

"Tonight," he promised, "we'll have the whole night together."

We waited for the woman who would preside over the marriage. Meanwhile, word had gotten around and people were calling to congratulate Azem. Unfortunately, it seemed that the Serbs had gotten wind of the wedding, too. Shells started to fall. The building shook from the explosions but we didn't care. It was a wedding, after all.

At the end of the ceremony, we all threw money at the couple. That was another Bosnian tradition. Usually at weddings, guests threw money and the couple and the children picked it up. Hard currency was rare and precious, so what we threw was the worthless currency from before the war. That had been Mirza's idea.

After the wedding, we went to a café. A popular singer, Nazif Gljiva, sang for the wedding party. Someone had procured a little meat which was rare as gold. Even a taste made for a feast.

We didn't dare stay together long since the café wasn't really secure. But for the time we were there, singing and drinking together, we briefly felt like people living normal lives.

Suljo and I left before the others so that we could spend some time alone. Making love was one thing that could make us forget the war and all the horrors around us.

"Jasmina," Suljo whispered that night, "I think we should make a baby. If I should die…"

"Suljo, you won't die. Don't say that. My baby is going to have a father who will love him and teach him about life."

"So you do want a baby?"

"Yes, yes! I want us to have a child."

"Jasmina, it will be the most beautiful baby in the world!"

We had always planned to have children one day. Ordinarily, we would have waited, but life in the siege was so precious and so uncertain that people didn't dare to put things off. Besides, it was true that Suljo could die. Of course, I didn't want to talk about it, but if it happened, I could at least have a baby to partly fill the empty place in my heart.

"Jasmina, I love you so much."

"And I love you."

Good news would alternate with the bad. One day when I was at work, someone called me from Central Bosnia.

"Are you Jasmina Ramic?"

"Yes, who is calling, please?"

"This is the hospital in Visoko. I'm calling to inform you that your sister-in-law, Rukija, delivered a healthy baby girl. Her name is Dalila. Congratulations!"

"Thank you! And how is Rukija?"

"Both she and her baby are doing well."

"No complications?" We had all worried because Rukija had been through so much in Visegrad. But Dalila arrived in perfect health and Rukija was just fine.

That was my mother's first grandchild. I wanted to be able to celebrate with Tajib. He was a daddy! But he was at the front lines that day.

Since I was bubbling over with happiness, I shared the news with the first people I could think of: the kitchen staff of the hospital.

"Hey, everyone! Tajib's wife had a baby!"

"Congratulations, Aunt Jasmina," said one of the cooks.

"We hope pretty soon you'll have a baby of your own."

The women in the kitchen adored Suljo and they had been thrilled at the news that we had decided to get pregnant. I got some coffee from the kitchen and took it upstairs to Ramo. He had been wounded in the leg and was recovering in a room above my office. Every day, I brought him coffee and a paper.

"Here's your coffee," I told him. "Today you don't need a newspaper because I'm delivering the news in person. Tajib's wife had a baby. They called me from Visoko."

"That's great! Tajib will be beside himself with joy."

Days later, though, we were grieving again. Our friend, Cazim, died. Like us, he was a refugee from Visegrad. He died fighting on the mountain, Trebevic, which overlooked Sarajevo. The Serbs held that mountain and the Bosnian Army had launched its newest offensive there.

Cazim was the first of many more deaths. Every day, I could see explosions on the side of that mountain. Suljo, two of my brothers and many of my friends were up there in the positions that the Serbs were shelling.

I learned of Cazim from Suljo. He had come down from the fighting to resupply.

"How about the others?" I asked him. "Are they all okay?"

"Five others died with Cazim," Suljo said. His face was white and his eyes looked dead. "A mortar exploded in our trench. I saw it all, Jasmina. I watched it happen. The shrapnel cut his head in two…"

He closed his eyes and I hugged him. I thought about Cazim's mother. How would they break the news to her? She had escaped from Visegrad where the Serbs had murdered her oldest son and her grandchild. Now she had lost her youngest son as well.

The offensive on Trebevic wore on. One day, much later, Suljo came to work to tell me his assignment had been changed. "We're going to Vogosca today," he said. "We'll be there six days."

"Have a cup of coffee with me," I said. "There's time for that, isn't there?"

My husband's face showed his exhaustion. "I can stay for half an hour. We're moving out in three hours and I have to get things ready."

I held him, not knowing if he would be back. I didn't even know if I would still be alive if he did return since the Serbs shelled the hospital so often. Periodically, a shell would penetrate and explode in a ward, killing doctors and the wounded.

There were many couples in the same situation as Suljo and me. One of the men who went to Vogosca with Suljo was Haris. A few days later, his wife, a nurse, was preparing wounded men for surgery. There was one man with a terrible head wound. Shrapnel had lodged in his brain and his face was covered with blood. The nurse had almost finished cleaning him up and getting him ready for the doctors before she realized that is was Haris, her husband. With all the blood, she hadn't even recognized him.

Emir Fejzic, too, was wounded at Vogosca. (I knew two young men named Emir. The one who visited me often in Buca Potok with Bahe and Tajib was never wounded, though both of his parents were killed in Visegrad.) When Seta came looking for the two wounded men, that was the first news I had from Vogosca. Obviously, the fighting was not going well there.

As I helped Seta to find out which clinics Haris and Emir were in, I thought about how Emir's family had tried to protect him from the news about his father. Emir didn't yet know that his father had been killed in Visegrad. Emir's mother had escaped but she hadn't told her son about his father because she knew he was going to fight soon. She was afraid that his grief would interfere. Now he might die anyway.

Haris's mother, too, had been killed in Visegrad. He had also lost a brother in Medjedja.

It got to me that day. I had to ask my boss for the rest of the day off. Then I walked to Buca Potok to be with my in-laws. They scolded me when I arrived. "Don't you see how bad the shooting is today?" And it was true. The walk to visit them had been dangerous. I had been the only person on the street but I needed to be with family.

"It's all right," I said. "I don't have to go to work tomorrow. I can stay here if the shelling is bad again tomorrow."

"When is Suljo coming? Did you hear anything from them?"

"They should be back tomorrow," I said.

I didn't tell my in-laws about Emir and Haris while Suljo was still away. It would only make my mother-in-law worry. I knew Suljo would come to Buca Potok when he heard that I was there. I needed his strong arms around me. I missed him so much. I stared out the window the next morning, hoping to see him walking up the street. Finally, I got tired of just sitting there and went to find something to do.

"Hello, Jasmina," said my uncle as he came into the house. "Will you give me something for a nice surprise? Suljo is right behind-"

I was out the door before he could finish his sentence. Suljo was just entering the yard.

"Oh, Suljo, I missed you so much! I've been worried!" He lifted me up and kissed me.

"I missed you," he said at last. "I picked some flowers for you at the front. I gave them to Sapko because I thought he would see you first. I hope he saved them. You won't believe the teasing I got when everyone saw me picking them for you."

We spent that day with Suljo's mother and father and grandmother. Then that evening, Suljo's mother insisted that we go visit Suljo's cousin, Nihad, and his wife, Elma. "They have water, electricity and a little extra space," my mother-in-law said. "You two should have some time to yourselves."

Nihad and Elma were happy to see us and delighted to share the boon of water and electricity. They had an empty floor in their house—the attic. Suljo and I realized that it was a dangerous place to stay the night but we didn't care. We wanted to be alone.

We took a shower together and played with the water. It's amazing how much pleasure you can find in something as simple as that, especially if you've been deprived of it. We had so much fun that we forgot the war for a few minutes.

When we were alone in the attic, it seemed a good time to tell Suljo that I had news for him.

His face was shining. "Tell me quick," he said. "Don't make me wait." I think he knew what I was going to say.

"I'm pregnant."

There was such joy in his eyes. I will never forget how he looked at that moment. I half expected him to sprout wings and fly around the room.

"I love you, Jasmina. When we leave here, I want you to quit working. It's too much stress. You'll come to Buca Potok to stay with my parents. You'll take care of yourself and they'll take care of you, too. And this will be the best baby in the whole world!"

"And you'll take care, too, won't you Suljo? I couldn't live without you." But then I didn't talk about that any more. This was a happy moment.

The next day, we had a vacation from the war and talk of war. Nihad and Elma had a ping-pong table. Suljo invited me to play but I said, "You and Nihad need the practice more than I do. Go ahead. After I'm done with the laundry, I'll show you both how the game is played."

I washed the clothes and helped Elma with lunch. The whole time, Suljo kept interrupting. "Come play with us, Jasmina! Don't be afraid to lose. It's only natural that we'll be better than you!"

"One game," I said, "just to put you in your place!"

I won but Suljo had lots of funny excuses for why he had lost.

An hour later, Tajib, Azem, Seta, Bahe, Emir Haskic and Ramo came to see us. We sat outside drinking coffee and telling stories. I couldn't recall when we'd last been together and had so much fun—some time in the distant past. I remembered that we'd have to leave the next day and I was sorry to have thought of that.

Azem remembered it, too. "Jasmina, you have to get back to work tomorrow and Suljo returns to duty. Do you want to come with us now?"

They had a car and going with them was much less dangerous than taking a bus or walking. But Suljo shook his head.

"We'll take the bus tomorrow," he said. He wanted one more night with real privacy.

"Whatever you want," Azem said. "I just think it's safer to come with us. You're sure?"

"Positive," said Suljo, taking my hand.

And that was our last night together.

Jasmina & Suljo in Sarajevo

24

Streets Painted with Blood

August 27th, 1992

I was very sorry when I heard the alarm clock go off the next morning. Our vacation from the war was over. I got up to make coffee and then I woke my husband.

"Come on, Suljo. We have to go." We said goodbye to Nihad and Elma.

As we walked to the bus stop, we heard birds singing. It was a beautiful day. August was always a wonderful time of year in Bosnia.

We teased each other, joking and laughing on our way. Before we knew it, we were at the bus stop. Very few people were there waiting.

"Suljo, I think we're too early." I glanced over at the wrist of a woman who was wearing a watch.

"It's ten past eight," she told me.

"Thank you."

We were twenty minutes early.

As we stood there, a UN armored vehicle came toward us on the street. Suljo was holding my hand and I squeezed his fingers. I was about to say that maybe we should move away from the armored car. United Nations vehicles sometimes drew fire from the Serbs.

Before I could say the words, we were flying.

That's what it felt like. Something had lifted us from the ground. I was aware of moving through the air before I heard the explosion. I distinctly heard Suljo call my name.

"Jasmina!"

I flew and then everything stopped. Everything went black.

I couldn't move at first.

I opened my eyes. Something had hit me. *What? What had happened?*

When I turned my head a little, I could see my right arm hanging by a thread from the bones of my shoulder. I could see there were bleeding holes in my legs. Deep holes. It seemed unreal, like I was looking at a picture.

I craned to look at Suljo. He hadn't said anything since he shouted my name.

There he was, right next to me.

His eyes were closed. His mouth was open a little. It looked like he was sleeping.

But when my eyes looked along the length of his body...I couldn't believe it was real. I couldn't believe it was happening.

I closed my eyes.

The right side of him was missing.

Oh, God, I thought, let this not be true. Let me wake up now. Let this be a horrible dream. Don't let my life with Suljo be over.

"Hurry! Hurry!" called a voice. "Oh my God! Oh my God, there are so many wounded!"

I opened my eyes again and saw the UN armored car pass

by. One of the blue-helmeted soldiers looked down but the vehicle rolled on without stopping. I could feel that I was getting weaker. My eyes closed again and I heard another voice say, "He's dead. So is she."

The voice was very close. He was talking about us. I pried my eyes open. A man in his sixties stood over us. He looked pale and shaken.

"I am not dead."

"She's still alive!" he shouted. "Hurry! Hurry!"

I couldn't manage to say anything more, though my eyes remained open. I could see the dead and wounded all around me. The man flagged down passing cars to take us to the hospital.

"Wounded first," I heard a different voice say. "We'll worry about the dead later."

It had been quiet in the first moments after the explosion but now I heard people screaming and sobbing. The street was painted with blood.

The man who had found me alive returned to me with two other men. They wrapped me in a blanket and carried me to one of the cars.

They put Suljo and another boy into the car with me and then we were jolting over the streets as fast as the driver dared to go. As we bounced over the pock-marked streets, pieces of my life with Suljo floated past me, one image at a time. I thought of how he had looked in the Drina, water streaming from his long hair on the day when I noticed him for the first time.

The driver pulled into what used to be a Yugoslav Army hospital.

"We'll take your dead," said a voice, "but we can't take any more wounded. These two will have to be transferred to Kosevo Hospital."

I felt myself blacking out. The sound of an explosion jolted me back to consciousness. I shouted, "You bastards! I'll screw your mothers!"

I blinked. I was in an ambulance now and there was a doctor next to me.

Another shell exploded.

"Damn you to hell, you bastards!"

I had never sworn like this in all my life. The doctor looked surprised, as if he'd given me up for dead.

I shouted obscenities a third time and the doctor smiled. "Listen to this!" I said. "Even now, they're shooting at us!" And I cursed them again. I kept up my shouting all the way to the hospital. I don't know where my strength came from—moments before I hadn't even been able to stay conscious.

The ambulance stopped and the doors opened. A doctor from the trauma center asked wearily, "How many?" The doctors at Kosevo often worked forty hours straight without rest. There were so many people who needed their attention. "How many are you bringing in?"

"About twenty," said the ambulance doctor.

"We don't have room for them in here. Take them to Orthopedics."

But every clinic was full. I knew, because it was my hospital. I worked there. The Orthopedic clinic took us anyway.

"Most critical first. The rest will have to wait."

They took me to the operating room. It was in the basement and had two operating tables. On the other table, they put the boy who had been carried with me and Suljo in the car.

I got my first good look at him. His face was familiar. He looked like he was about fifteen. He was shaking and whenever he screamed his whole body went rigid. "Don't cut off my leg!" he pleaded. "Don't cut my leg!"

His leg, like my right arm, was hanging by a thread of tissue.

Then I remembered where I knew him from. He had recently been in the hospital with a broken arm.

I felt cold, like my bones had turned to ice. I was beginning to feel pain. I guess I had been too traumatized to feel it before then.

"Can you give me something for the pain?"

"You've got to tell us your name before we put you under," a doctor declared in a loud voice. "Who are you?"

"Jasmina Ramic."

"Was anybody with you when this happened?"

"Yes. My husband was with me. He died. They left him at the other hospital. I work here. I was coming to work."

They looked at me as if I were delirious. As they prepared to operate on me, they asked the same questions again and again to see if I was coherent.

"I told you. I'm Jasmina Ramic. My husband died right next to me, I saw him. My brother is Zenga. Call him. Please call my brother."

Everyone knew who Azem was. When they called him, he would be able to answer all their questions.

And then I had no more strength. Everything went black and I was nothing.

25

Dr. Ismet

I woke up in intensive care. My right arm had been amputated at the shoulder. My legs were covered in bandages and my face felt strange. My nose was swollen and I could see something black on it. There were all sorts of tubes and devices attached to me. I couldn't move.

Azem was in the room with me, along with his friends, Dr. Cibo, who I knew from work, and Kina. Kina and Azem had been wounded in the same firefight and met at the hospital. Kina was now the commander of the boys—very young Bosnian soldiers—who guarded the hospital and made visitors check their weapons before entering.

My boss, Faruk, came in, too, when they sent word that I was waking up.

There were tears in Faruk's eyes as he looked at me in the bed.

"Hey, Faruk. I wanted to come to work. See? I got here." I didn't want him to cry. My joke fell flat. He said nothing but leaned over the bed and kissed my forehead. Azem had left the room. I guess my brother didn't want to cry in front of me. He came back a few minutes later and suddenly something gave way in me. I couldn't be strong any longer. I couldn't keep my feelings hidden.

"Suljo!" I wailed. "Suljo, Suljo!"

I kept keening his name. I'm sure people could hear me through half the hospital. No one in the room tried to stop me until a nurse came over from another part of the ward. "Jasmina, don't," she said. "You can't do this to yourself. You have to put what's in the past behind you and concentrate all your effort on healing."

I looked at Azem. He was sobbing.

"I don't care about me," I said. "I don't want to live without Suljo."

The look in Azem's eyes made me regret that as soon as I said it. Wasn't he hurting enough? I hadn't meant to salt his wounds.

"I'm glad I survived," I said. "I'm glad I'll be able to see our mother again."

"Jasmina, you will see her. I promise I'll find a way for you to see her."

A young doctor came into the room. He was smiling. "Jasmina! My champion! I'm glad to see you awake. I'm Ismet Gavrankapetanovic. I'm the one who operated on you and we should congratulate each other. We lost you on the operating table. The anesthesiologist didn't want to give you anesthesia because he thought there was no saving you. But I brought you back and you didn't let me down!"

I liked him instantly. There was something irresistible about his smile. Underneath his joviality was a concern that reached deep inside of me and cradled my pain.

"Soon, I'm going to introduce you to a couple girls your age," he went on. "They're in another ward. After a while, I expect you to be able to move in with them."

"Doctor, what's wrong with my nose? I can't breathe."

"We've got you packed full of cotton. Some shrapnel tore through your nose but I sewed you back together and you'll be fine. I did a good job for you."

"Thank you, Doctor. Thank you very much."

Tajib and my friends arrived then to see me. The area around my bed was getting crowded and Dr. Gavrankapetanovic teased me. "This is intensive care, you know, not City Central. If you keep attracting visitors like this, we're going to have to move you to another ward!"

Of the visits I received on that first day, the one that was hardest on me was Sapko's. He joined my friends and family, bearing a bouquet of wilted flowers.

"Jasmina," he said, "Suljo picked these for you at the front line. He asked me to bring them to you. I thought...I was sure you'd still want them, even though they are fading."

Again, I wanted to die. How could I live without Suljo? I called to him, pleading for him to come back. "Suljo, my Suljo!" I wanted my husband to kiss me. I wanted to feel his strong arms around me. I wanted to see him smile and tell me how much he loved me.

No one could console me. Soon I was screaming his name. "Suljo! Suljo!"

This time, even the nurses who tried to comfort me began to cry.

When my father-in-law came to visit, everyone else in the room likely expected him to burst into tears. He was a very tender-hearted man who had lost his only son. Instead, he stood silently at the side of my bed looking into my eyes. We didn't have to talk. We each knew how much Suljo had meant to the other.

He started to lift the sheets that covered me. "Father, I don't have any clothes on!"

"It doesn't matter. You're my child. They told me you were wounded in the belly and I wanted to see if it was true."

"No, Father, I'm not wounded there. I have some wounds in my back, from the force of the explosion."

"Suljo told me that you were pregnant. I was worried about the baby."

"I didn't know he'd told you that. But don't worry. I'll give my last breath to keep our baby safe."

I didn't know when Suljo could have told his father that I was pregnant but I wasn't really surprised. My father-in-law loved children and he'd been looking forward to being a grandfather. His daughter wasn't able to have children so his hopes were with me and Suljo.

When I asked my doctor about the baby, he said it was too early to know anything. That made me sad. I wanted to know immediately that Suljo's baby would be all right and I told him so. He advised me not to worry.

26

The Will to Survive

The hospital never slept. Around two in the morning, the doctors chased away Katarina, Azem and Senada. But even alone, I couldn't sleep. I could hear the cries of other patients.

Not long before dawn, I heard screaming.

"My legs! My legs are killing me!" someone screamed in agony. His cries got louder and louder. The doctors were bringing him into intensive care.

The sound of his cries was piercing. It drove me mad. The only thing I could move was my head. I could face away from the direction of his screaming but that was all I could do.

They put him in the bed next to mine. "My legs! My legs!"

There were several people around him. One of the nurses said to me, "He's wounded in the stomach. He doesn't know what he's talking about."

She was very cold about it but I could understand that. She

saw nothing but horrors, day in and day out. It would be too much to ask her to keep feeling.

I could sympathize with the man, though. Lying in the street, I hadn't known where I was wounded until I had seen my injuries with my own eyes.

His screaming continued for ten minutes. Then, rather suddenly, he stopped.

"Did he fall asleep?" I asked the nurse. "He's dead," she told me.

I watched them take him out of the room. It seemed almost an ordinary thing to me, the sudden way people died.

The next day was Suljo's funeral. I was the only one who had to miss it, who couldn't say goodbye to him. It wasn't fair.

All I could do was look out the window in the direction of the sports stadium which had been converted into a graveyard. That's where they had taken him. Soon, even the stadium grounds would be too crowded with the dead.

I could see that the area around the stadium was being shelled. The Serbs just never let up. I worried for my family and friends.

Dr. Gavrankapetanovic interrupted my thoughts. "Hi, Jasmina. How are you today? We're going to change your bandages now and check your wounds."

He was smiling. He managed always to be smiling. I didn't know how he could do it. I always felt better when I saw him. "Hello, Doctor. I'm all right, I guess. My husband's funeral is today and I can't even be there to tell him goodbye."

"I'm sorry, Jasmina. But let's think about the future! I've got good news about your future roommates. I told them all about you and they're dying to meet you. Pretty soon, we'll get you moved out of here."

"What are their names?"

"Zeljka and Mihreta. You'll like them, I know."

He was still smiling. I felt I had known Dr. Gavrankapetanovic for years.

A nurse came in with all the supplies needed to change my bandages.

"Okay," said the doctor. "First your shoulder."

He unwrapped my bandages and started to clean my shoulder. The nerves of my wound were raw and every time he swabbed the area it felt as though he were scrubbing away my flesh. The longer he worked, the more it hurt.

"You can bite down on the sheets," the nurse suggested. I wadded up a corner of the sheet and stuffed it into my mouth. Every time the doctor cut or swabbed, I clenched my jaw as tightly as I could. Tears rolled down my cheeks. I wanted the torture to end but it went on and on.

I let the sheet fall out of my mouth and shouted, "Stop! Doctor, I can't take this!"

"I know how much this hurts, Jasmina. But your wounds are dirty and I can't sew them up before I clean them. We don't have the antibiotics we need. This is the only way. If we don't go through with this, you could die."

"I don't care. Just leave me. What do I have to live for, anyway?"

"Jasmina, I know that you're stronger than your words." He kept right on working while he talked. "I'm going to finish cleaning your shoulder." He was cutting. I winced, but kept silent. "Then I'm going to clean your legs. It will hurt but it won't go on forever. When it's done, you'll sleep better."

Soon he had finished with my shoulder. When he pulled the sheets back from my legs, I lifted my head to see my wounds clearly for the first time.

I wasn't prepared for what I saw. I had seen countless wounded people and many, many shrapnel injuries. But I had never seen anything like my own legs. There were six gaping holes in my flesh. I could see down to bone.

"Oh, my God! My legs!"

"I know it looks bad, Jasmina," said the doctor. He got right to work so that my ordeal would be over as soon as possible. "We're going to get you fixed up, though. You know, you lost so much blood that your heart stopped. But here you are. You're a survivor. You aren't going to let me down and give up now. No, you're not."

The pain was excruciating and made worse by the fact that I could now see a little of what he was doing. I turned my face away but he kept up his encouraging words.

"Come on, Jasmina. Staying alive is a good start but now you have to decide to keep living."

I wasn't sure if I wanted that. I wasn't sure that I cared. But he cared. I found myself wanting to do as he said, just for the sake of showing my gratitude for his words.

From that day, Dr. Gavrankapetanovic never let anyone else change my bandages even though the nurses were perfectly capable. He wanted to do it himself, to talk me through the pain. That was half of what kept me alive. The other half was the visits of friends and family.

After the funeral, everyone came to see me.

"Jasmina, what do you want?" Tajib asked me. "Your brother will bring you anything you want. Anything. That's not easy in a war, you know." He smiled, trying to cheer me up. "You want ice cream? Chocolates?"

"Tajib, I can't eat. I'll drink some coffee, though. My head is killing me."

He brought me coffee. Then I asked him about Suljo's funeral.

"A lot of people were there," he said. "Did you see Suljo?"

"Yes," Tajib said quietly. "I saw him."

I was crying and I couldn't stop. I still couldn't believe Suljo was dead and I kept hoping that it would all turn out to be a bad dream.

My father-in-law walked into the room with Nihad and Suljo's uncle. I could see from their faces that they had been crying. Soon, tears were streaming down their faces again.

When Katarina joined us, she brought along Terry, a French journalist we knew, and some other friends from the Belgrade Hotel. She also brought a letter from the children who lived in the hotel.

"Dear Jasmina," they wrote, "We are very sorry about Suljo. We know how much you loved him and how you must feel now. You're his girl, though, and you must remember to be strong for him and for your love. We love you. We will always be your friends."

They had all signed their names and sent a flower along with the letter. The children of the siege were amazing. In many respects, they couldn't be children any more. They would sometimes get to play but the main thing in their lives was war. They had to grow up and take life seriously. War changed all of us but it affected the children most of all.

Terry had brought me some medicine and some sweets. For the sake of my baby, I didn't want to use the medicine so I later gave it to the nurse to use in the children's ward. As for the candies, I didn't much feel like eating anything and I knew that the children on the hospital's second floor would be delighted with such a treat. I told Katarina to take it to them.

When Katarina returned, she said, "I told those children all about you, Jasmina. They want to see you now, so when you can sit in a wheelchair, I'll take you up to visit them."

I liked the thought of visiting the children but when would I be able to sit up? I was attached to so much medical machinery that I couldn't move and my legs were useless. When the nurses changed my sheets, five of them had to lift me up while another switched the sheets beneath me. I was stuck in the same position all the time. When I wanted to move my legs from one position to another, I had to call a nurse to come do it for me.

"I don't see how I'll ever walk again," I told the nurse one time. "I can't even move my legs a little bit."

"Of course you're discouraged," she said. "But in a few days, you won't have to call me. You'll move your legs on your own and then we'll see about getting you to walk."

"Walk on what? Look down there! There's nothing to hold me up!"

"Nurse?" called another patient. "Can you come here for a second?"

In intensive care, the nurses were always being called from one patient to the other or were making the rounds among the patients who couldn't call to them. Everyone was in need of something. We were all helpless to some degree. It didn't do much to give me hope, seeing how many of us had lost pieces of ourselves inside and out.

There were eight of us in intensive care. Across from me was a fireman who had lost an arm while fighting a fire. He had internal injuries as well and his leg had been mangled. He was about thirty years old.

The girl next to me was my age. Her limbs were intact but she'd been horribly wounded in the stomach. Across from her was an old man who had big holes in his belly. He urinated and defecated through those holes. That was a terrible sight.

Next to the old man was the young boy who had lost his leg. Listening to his screams as his bandages were changed was the worst part of my stay in intensive care. It was worse than my own pain and was part of why I fought so hard to bear my own pain in silence.

After a few days, I was moved from intensive care to a regular room with the girls my doctor had told me about. Zeljka and Mihreta were sweet and cheerful, though what mattered more to me at the time was that I was getting out of intensive care.

Tajib, Katarina and many of my friends were there when I was moved. Dr. Gavrankapetanovic pushed my bed to the new room and my friends brought along my things.

"Zeljka, Mihreta," said my doctor, "this is your new roommate and friend, Jasmina."

Both women looked like they were about my age or a little older.

"Hey, Jasmina!" Mihreta said. "Welcome to our room. The doctor and Benjamin told us all about you."

Benjamin was a friend of Azem's whom I had met in the hospital. Benjamin had come to visit his father, the popular singer, Safet Isovic. Safet was also one of Azem's friends. He had been sitting on the balcony of his house one day when a shell exploded in his house. The blast had flayed all the flesh from his back.

"Welcome, Jasmina," said Zeljka. "How are you?"

"Unhappy because, you know, I lost my husband," I said. "But otherwise, I'm okay."

It was a stupid thing to say. Obviously I wasn't okay. I probably looked more dead than alive. I was still refusing to eat. Everyone pleaded with me to eat but I couldn't bear food. Suljo was on my mind all of the time. He was all I thought of and my eyes always felt puffy from crying.

"Okay," said my doctor, "thanks for helping Jasmina move, everyone. But now you've got to go. It's time for me to change her bandages."

"Not again!" I said to him. "I'll kill myself!"

"Out, everyone, please," the doctor said, herding my family and friends out the door. "You can come again to visit her this evening." He never let anyone but other patients stay in the room when he changed my bandages.

"When are you going to sew me up?" I pleaded. "I can't take more of this!"

"As soon as we can," Dr. Gavrankapetanovic promised. "Just think about how much better you always feel an hour after your wounds have been cleaned. We'll do your legs first today because we have to clean a little deeper."

He was worried about gangrene. Instead of sewing me up right away, he was delaying it and cutting off any flesh that appeared to be going rotten. He couldn't offer me anesthesia—there was only enough anesthetic for patients undergoing surgery.

There are no adequate words to describe what it's like to have your body scraped and cut away in little bits at a time. It was agonizing. But my doctor at least tried to help me through it with his stream of encouraging words. Every moment of the cleaning felt like torture but his words were all to remind me that it was not torture, it was his effort to care for me, to heal me.

The doctor arranged my legs. I covered my face with the pillow because I couldn't stand the sight of the holes.

"Sabina," he said to the nurse, "give me the scissors."

"Scissors?" I took the pillow away. He had never asked for scissors before. "What are you going to do?"

"Jasmina, I'm sorry, but you have large areas where the flesh has died. It will rot if we don't remove it and the infection could kill you. We have to protect the healthy muscle that remains. Do you want to ever walk again? Then you're going to have to be very strong, hold very still and help me do this for you. All right?"

I nodded.

"I really do mean that you have to help me. You have to guide me. When the pain is the worst you have ever felt, you tell me. The condition of your nerves will help me know where to cut."

His smile made me brave. I trusted him. I put the sheets into my mouth.

He started to cut and it hurt. I wanted to scream but bit down on the sheets instead. This was just the usual pain. From what he'd said, it would get worse.

I was sweating. The sheets beneath me were wet. "It hurts a lot!" I said.

"Good girl. Just hang in there. Be strong."

After an eternity of snipping and scraping, he started to work on my shoulder. As he worked, I could hear the scissors open and close. I thought it would have been better to die in the explosion. This was worse than death. I wanted to thrash against the pain and scream. Instead, I bit down harder on the sheets. I ground my teeth, shredding the cotton fabric.

The nurse said, "Doctor, I'm sorry. I have to get out." Her face was yellow and she was as drenched in sweat as I was.

She hurried from the room.

"I want to die!" I screamed. "Stop!"

"Almost finished," said Dr. Gavrankapetanovic. "The two of us are amazing together, don't you think? We don't need anybody to help us, do we? Tell me about your brother. How is Zenga doing these days?"

I concentrated on his questions. We talked about my family while he went on cutting. For all his efforts to distract me, the pain grew steadily worse.

"Done!" he said at last. "For today, we are done. Now you can rest."

I managed to say, "Thank you, doctor."

Zeljka and Mihreta were pale and shaking. They looked as if they had just been subjected to my agonies. They had just met me. This was the first time they had seen the extent of my wounds. It was also the last. After that, they always left the room when Dr. Gavrankapetanovic came to change my bandages.

"Things will get better," Dr. Gavrankapetanovic said.

It was hard to believe him. It was hard to think of a life without Suljo that was worth that kind of pain. For consolation, I thought of how much I wanted to see my mother again and I thought of Suljo's baby. Those were reasons to take one more breath and then one more. But with the exception of those events glimmering in a distant future, my nights and days alike were black and bitter.

27

Helping Each Other

In truth, there were many lights that led me out of the darkness.

My roommates, Zeljka and Mihreta, persisted in talking to me, drawing me out. Zeljka had lost one leg and she had serious injuries to her other leg and one arm. She had been smoking a cigarette with some friends in front of her building when a shell came down in their midst. Two of her friends died and the others were as badly wounded as she was. Zeljka was twenty-three years old and very beautiful. Her dark hair and complexion made her look exotic.

Mihreta was twenty-eight but she looked more like she was my age. She was married but didn't have any children. She was a solider and had been shot by a sniper at the front line. She looked like a soldier—very strong. She played recorded music and sang to it. Right from the start, she invited me to sing along with her.

During the day, Zeljka and Mihreta worked to cheer me up. Daytime was easier than the night. I could talk about Suljo while the sun was shining and not feel completely overwhelmed with grief. But at night, when my roommates were asleep and my family and friends were gone, I looked out of the dark window and all I could see was Suljo's mutilated body lying in the street. I would hear again the voices of the wounded, the barely controlled panic of those strangers who stopped to help us. And I heard, again and again, the last time that Suljo called out my name.

At those times, I would cry out, "Lela! Lela!"

Lela was the night nurse. I would try not to call for her if I could help it. I knew she had others to attend to. But often I couldn't bear the darkness, couldn't bear being alone with my memories.

"Jasmina, I'm here," she would say. "Do you need anything?"

"I'm scared. I can't sleep. Lela, every time I close my eyes, I see it all again. I hear their voices. I'm so afraid."

"It's all right. I'm right here." She would ask me to tell her about my life before the war. She asked me all about Suljo, about what kind of man he had been.

When I talked to Lela, it was like bringing Suljo back for a little while. I could almost forget that I was in the hospital. And I lost track of how helpless I felt. If I still couldn't sleep, we talked together until the sun came up. In the morning, when Zeljka and Mihreta had woken up, my friends and family would come visit.

I hated to be alone and Lela was my companion through my hardest hours.

I didn't always know the people who encouraged me. One morning after a long night talking to Lela, a young boy in a wheelchair rolled into our room. He was barely a teenager. Looking at him, I thought of my brother Samir. Tears began to well up in my eyes.

This boy steered his wheelchair to my bed.

"Hi, Jasmina," he said. "Katarina told me about you. She said you can't sit in a wheelchair so I came to visit you. My name is Samir."

My heart skipped a beat. He not only reminded me of my murdered brother, he had the same name.

"So how are you today?"

"I'm all right," I said. "How are you, Samir?"

"Okay. My operations are finished and I'll walk in a few days. My brother isn't doing so well. He lost a leg and both his arms are wounded. He's like you. He can't be in a wheelchair yet."

"I'm sorry. Tell me about your brother. How old is he?"

"His name is Damir. We're twins. We're both thirteen years old."

I started to cry. Samir looked concerned and I tried to stop sobbing. "My brother's name was Samir. The Serbs killed him in Visegrad. He also had a twin, my brother Almir. Almir is still alive, thank God."

"I'm sorry for your brother," Samir said. "But try not to cry. You have to be strong. If you want to get better and walk again, you have to think about what lies in the future, not about the things that have already happened. When you're feeling stronger, we'll get you into a wheelchair and then you can come visit us in the children's ward. What do you think?"

"I think that would be very nice, Samir."

I couldn't believe he was thirteen. He seemed more wise and caring than some men were at fifty.

"I have to go now," he said, "before the doctors make their rounds." The doctors came by every morning at about ten o'clock to check on their patients. Before then, the nurses helped us brush our teeth, wash our faces and change our sheets if there were any freshly cleaned ones available. Since the hospital often went many weeks without water, clean sheets were a rare luxury. Samir said, "See ya!"

"Thank you for coming, Samir. It was very nice to talk to you. Say hello to your brother from me and tell him that I'm going to come to visit."

When my doctor met me on his rounds, I was still thinking of Samir and his wounded twin. I wanted to see all the children. When Dr. Gavrankapetanovic appeared in our ward, I asked him when I'd be able to sit in a wheelchair.

"Well," he said, "why don't we see? Today we'll get a nurse to help you stand and we'll find out if you can manage it."

"Please, not with the nurse. I want to wait until Tajib comes today. He can help me."

"Okay," Dr. Gavrankapetanovic said. "That's fine." Half an hour later, Tajib and my friends arrived.

"Jasmina," my brother said, "we found you some meat so you've got to eat it."

I had lost a lot of weight but I still couldn't eat. The thought of food sickened me.

"I'll have some coffee," I said.

"No, you can't survive forever on just coffee."

"I don't want to eat. The doctor told me I can try to stand up today, though. I've been waiting for you. I only want to try with your help."

I loved all my brothers and sisters but Tajib was the oldest and my favorite. With his help, I thought I might not only walk, but fly.

He got mad at me, though. "Jasmina, if you don't eat anything, how are you ever going to walk? You've got to eat to go on living. Do you understand that?"

I started to cry. "I can't eat." But I knew I had to.

Tajib lifted me from the bed like a baby and put me in his lap.

"Mince, we'll try to get you to stand. But then you'll try to eat, okay? Would the doctor let you try to stand if he knew you hadn't eaten anything?"

Tajib put my feet on the floor and held me up. I couldn't feel the weight of my body, couldn't feel the floor against the bottoms of my feet. The room started spinning. I fought to hide my dizziness from Tajib and gathered every bit of strength in order to take a step.

But I couldn't move.

"You look like you're about to faint," Tajib said. "Do you want me to put you back in the bed?"

I tried and tried but I couldn't get my legs to even twitch. I couldn't feel them at all.

"Okay," I said. "Put me back."

"Now you see," Tajib said as he lifted me into the bed. "Now you understand why you have to eat. You've got to get your strength back."

Katarina made some soup in the hospital's kitchen and they fed it to me.

I felt like a baby. I couldn't walk, I couldn't feed myself and I couldn't even go to the bathroom on my own. The nurses had to bring me a bedpan and lift me up to use it. It was humiliating. I suppose it was another thing that motivated me, the shame of being so helpless.

My family and friends were trying so hard to do everything they could for me. It was Zeljka who really brought home to me how precious they were. One day, as shells were falling near the hospital, she just started crying.

"What is it?" I asked her.

"I was thinking of Sarajevo before the war," she said. "I was thinking about the discos. I loved dancing and now I'll never be able to dance again." She paused. "No, that's not what hurts me. Jasmina, you lost a lot, but you still have dear brothers who would do anything for you and you have Katarina and so many friends. You'll never be alone. I don't have any brothers or sisters and my mother has been sick for almost two years now. She's been in the hospital all that time. My father is getting old and he can barely take care of himself."

"Zeljka, you aren't alone. We're sisters now, you, me and Mihreta. We'll never let you be alone. My brothers will do all they can for you, too."

Mihreta's scream cut our conversation short.

"I'm sorry," she said. "My leg hurts. God, I'm in such pain!"

She got up and walked around the room with her crutches. The shells were hitting the hospital by then. We all felt scared and we were about to holler for the nurse to get us out of the room when we heard singing.

There were two voices, a man's and a woman's. Their voices were beautiful and getting louder.

My friend, Benjamin, appeared in the doorway. "Jasmina, some people have come to see you."

Behind Benjamin came two Bosnian singers, Hanka Paldum and Meho Puzic. They came over to my bed.

"Jasmina, we know how badly you must feel. You've lost so much and that's why we want to sing for you. Songs always help."

"They're going to the front lines, too," Benjamin said, "to sing for the soldiers."

I was proud of my country and my people. They weren't giving up. No matter how bad things got, no matter who refused to help them, they got right back on their own feet. Singers entertaining at the front lines! That's who we were, that was the Bosnian people.

"Benjamin, I want to sit up to listen to them. Put me in the wheelchair."

Benjamin found a wheelchair and lifted me from the bed. Sitting in the wheelchair was hard, though. I couldn't bend my knees, so Benjamin arranged pillows under my legs to keep them straight. The singers sat on my bed and started to sing a duet.

They had strong voices. Everyone in the whole clinic—and maybe even in other clinics—could hear them. Patients from other parts of the building came to our room, drawn by the singing.

Hanka Paldum and Meho Puzic were right. Songs did help, especially when we all began to sing together. The shelling continued but so did our singing.

My doctor appeared in our room when this was going on. When he saw me sitting in a wheelchair for the first time, singing, he smiled his miracle smile. I smiled back.

"How long can you sit in a wheelchair?" he asked.

"I'm very tired but when they sing I don't feel it as much. You know, they should come sing when you change my bandages."

"Did you eat anything?"

"Yes."

"Excellent. Maybe in a few days, we'll sew up your wounds."

"You're a second father to me, Doctor. My parents brought me into this world the first time. I think you brought me into it the second time."

He laughed. "Together," he said, "we're a team."

If there was one single event that transformed me, that evening of singing was it. When the singers had left and the war came crashing in on us again, I was ready to handle it.

The shelling outside had meant casualties. One was a girl who was screaming as they brought her into our room. I tried to see her face to get an idea of how old she was but it was night by then and the hospital was without electricity. I couldn't see her.

Sejo, a medical technician, was asking her the usual questions. He finally got her calmed down some.

"What's your name?"

"Narima Turcilo," she said. "They call me Mima."

"Where did this happen to you, Mima?"

"Near my building. I was with my friend when the sniper shot me."

"Where do you live?"

"In Vojnicko Polje."

Vojnicko Polje was one of the worst parts of Sarajevo. The Serbs held positions very close by and there were many people who were shot there every day by snipers. "Mima, how old are you?"

"I'm seventeen."

"Who should we contact about this? Should we call your father to tell him you're here?"

"My father's dead. You can call my brother."

Sejo left the room to call. As soon as he had gone, she started to scream again. I guessed that she screamed as much out of fear as from pain. She was afraid of the hospital.

"Mima," I said to her, "don't scream. It's all right. I know this seems like a terrible place, but it's not. You're with friends. I'm Jasmina and the other women here are Zeljka and Mihreta. We have a good time. We were scared at first, too, but now we have each other."

"You're going to be all right," Mihreta said.

"Hi," said Zeljka. "Everybody is afraid on the first day. It's okay."

"See?" I said. "You're in good company."

Helping each other, I began to realize, was an important step in helping ourselves.

After her first bad night, Mima settled in as well as anyone could be expected to. Soon the four of us were good friends, telling each other the stories of our lives.

We tried to find small ways to make ourselves happy. When there was electricity, we played music as loud as the nurses let us and turned the room into a disco. We sang and moved whatever parts of our bodies would move, pretending to dance. Our room became a social hub. Patients from other parts of the hospital came to listen to our music or play cards. Even playing cards was a challenge with missing or damaged limbs but we really wanted to play and socialize, so we managed. If you want something badly enough, you figure out how to overcome the challenges. For me, the biggest challenge was staying in the wheelchair to play for hours at a time. My knees still would not bend.

Helping others was what kept me going. Terry, the French journalist, brought me some more candy and for the first time, I was able to take it to the children myself. Some of the kids I visited hadn't seen candy since the war started which kept me from eating even one piece. Katarina put me in a wheelchair and placed the candy in my lap.

When we got to the second floor, I realized—too late—that I wasn't ready to see it.

There were babies and toddlers on the ward who didn't have legs, arms or eyes. They had barely come into this world and had become victims of the madness that even grown-ups couldn't understand. Katarina and I happened to arrive as nurses were changing bandages. The children were shrieking with pain and fear. I at least knew what was happening to me and why. Having wounds cleaned without anesthetic must have been so much worse for the children. To them, it was torture.

Some of the children were orphans. Some were the children of soldiers, men and women who couldn't be with their babies because someone had to serve at the front lines.

I thought of all the families separated, the children without their parents. I thought of my own father in a Serb concentration camp. What was happening to him there? I worried about how my mother was holding up. The telephones worked so seldom, I hadn't been able to talk to her.

Katarina noticed my expression. "The nurses will finish changing the bandages soon," she said, "then we can give the children the candy."

Candy was so little to give. It was such a meager offering. Katarina saw how the sights and sounds of the ward made me suffer but what she couldn't know was what it felt like to lose family, pieces of one's body and any measure of self-reliance, all at once. I knew what these children were going through and I resolved to come visit them whenever I could.

As it turned out, the candy thrilled them. In some ways, children are more resilient than adults. Once their bandages had been changed, the children were able to receive our simple gift with happiness. That day marked us as special visitors. From then on, Katarina and I arrived on the children's ward as celebrities. Every time we came, the children yelled, "Zenga's sister and Zenga's wife are here!"

Samir, who had visited me in his wheelchair, became my special friend, along with Damir, his brother. Damir was still confined to his bed.

Another special child was Indira, a three-year-old girl. She had lost her leg as her father was carrying her to a basement bomb shelter. Her father had been killed.

I loved Indira's spirit. She wanted to walk and play as much as any child. Her mother taught her to walk with crutches but she got around as much as she could without them. She wanted to be normal. I wanted that for her, too. She was one of the lucky ones to be evacuated from Sarajevo to a better hospital, one with electricity and running water and no daily barrage of explosive shells.

But though Indira got out of Sarajevo, her little bed did not go unused. As soon as she was gone, another wounded child took her place.

Finally, even anger and grief became my allies.

One day, around one a.m., the Serbs were really pounding the hospital. Patients had all been brought to the basement or were lined up in the interior hallways, away from the outer walls.

My three roommates and I were next to each other in the dark hall. The shelling was getting to me that night. I closed my eyes tightly to make it even darker. I wished there were some way to shut out the sounds as well—I couldn't help hearing the whistles and explosions of falling shells. The whistle was the first warning you had that shells were coming down but you wouldn't hear the sound in time to save yourself if the shell was coming right at you.

All of a sudden, I heard a voice like Bahe's. I looked around, then realized it couldn't be him, of course. He was with Azem on the front line. Only Tajib had stayed behind to look after me and the wounded soldiers from their brigade. I closed my eyes again.

Someone took my hand. It was Bahe.

"Bahe, how come you're here?"

"Goga and Sapko are wounded. We brought them in a little while ago. They're in surgery now. We're waiting for them to come out."

"How are they? Are they seriously wounded?"

"They have all their limbs but they have bad internal wounds, Sapko more than Goga."

Before long we heard Goga's screams. The nurses were bringing him from surgery to his room and he was screaming just as Mima had done when she was first brought in.

"Water!" he pleaded with the nurses. "Give me some water, please! I want to have some water!"

But he'd just come out of surgery. He wouldn't be allowed anything to eat or drink right away. The nurses put him in a room down the hall from us. All night long, I heard his screams and pleas.

Bahe asked the nurse about Sapko. She said he was in intensive care.

In the morning, Tajib came by very early with Suljo's family. It was usually the best part of the day when they all came to see me. My mother-in-law always brought me clean sheets. She brought clean underwear, too, so that I could change every day. There were so many things I couldn't do for myself but I had lots of friends who washed my hair or changed my underwear for me.

Sometimes my mother-in-law brought clean sheets for Zeljka, too, since she didn't have anyone to wash her sheets. And my mother-in-law also brought fresh food for the four of us. I still wasn't eating much. I wanted to get better but food didn't appeal to me. I could still only eat by an act of will.

"I want to go see Goga and Sapko," I told my in-laws. We went to see Goga first. He wasn't feeling well. He was crying and it was hard to see such a strong and brave soldier cry. Sooner or later, though, what you saw of the war would get to you.

He stopped crying when he saw me. "Jasmina, how can you smile? You're wounded so much worse than I am and yet you keep on smiling."

Smiling and feeling hopeful had become a duty to me. That's because the nurses had made such an example of me, telling other patients, "Look at Jasmina. She can take it. So can you." Once you become an example, you want to keep it up.

"I can sing, too," I said, grinning at him. "When you can sing, you'll know you're getting better." Actually, it wasn't easy to smile for Goga after seeing him cry.

"I'm worried about my children," he said. "Who will bring them food while I'm in the hospital?"

"You have good friends. You have your family. They'll care for your children. Right now, your concern is to make yourself strong."

If smiling for Goga was hard, it was ten times harder to smile when I saw Sapko. I didn't even try. He'd been seriously wounded in the stomach and leg. He couldn't talk or even keep his eyes open. His face was yellow and I was afraid for him.

"Will he be all right?" I asked the intensive care nurse. "Don't worry, Jasmina," she said. "If you survived, it's guaranteed that he will, too."

Seeing the young men in those states made me angry. Why did this have to happen?

Back in my room, my in-laws and I talked about how safe we'd thought Sarajevo would be. It was the city where the world had come for the Olympics. People from all over the globe had seen and appreciated the beauty of this place and we'd felt so sure that they would not stand to see it reduced to rubble.

But rubble it was. The buildings that hadn't been pounded to stones and dust had big holes punched in them. And the shells kept falling.

The next morning, a bomb fell in front of our clinic and a few more people died. Two nurses were wounded.

All of this was on my mind: Goga, Sapko, the destruction

of the city, the world's indifference, the people killed and the nurses wounded. Those were the things I was stewing about when Sejo, the medical technician, nudged me and said, "Jasmina! Wake up and lift your legs!"

Sejo had been urging me every day to move my legs, without success. But on that day, I was so angry and so distracted that I didn't think about what I couldn't do. I lifted my leg for the first time.

Then I stared at my leg. I couldn't believe it. "Sejo, look! I lifted my leg by myself!"

Sejo, Zeljka, Mihreta and Mima all started to cheer.

I could hardly wait for Tajib and my doctor to come see me that day. I watched the door eagerly. As soon as I saw Tajib, I lifted my leg and kept it raised for as long as I could.

Tajib smiled the biggest smile. His eyes lit up. He came to my bed and lifted me into his lap. "Mince, I'm so happy! You'll try to walk again today but only after you eat something."

He found a wheelchair, propped up my stiff legs and wheeled me to Goga's room. Goga and I ate together. I actually felt hungry. For the first time, food appealed to me again.

After I ate, Tajib wheeled me back to my room. Then he took me out of the wheelchair and, standing in front of me, supported my waist with his hands.

"Okay, let's first see if you can just stand."

This time, I could feel the weight of my body on the bottoms of my feet. I didn't feel dizzy. Tajib gradually lessened his support on my hips.

I was standing!

I took a deep breath and I shifted my weight. I willed my leg forward.

I took a step.

Tajib smiled and I tried for another step. I shifted my weight and moved my other leg.

"How are you feeling?" Tajib said. "Tired? Okay?"

"Let's keep going!" I said.

I took another tiny step…and then another.

That day, for the first time after a month in the hospital, I walked from my bed to the door with Tajib helping to support me. Dr. Gavrankapetanovic came into the room as I took the last few steps. For a moment, he was so surprised that he forgot his smile. I realized then that he hadn't expected me to ever walk again.

He recovered his smile. "Jasmina, you're ready for another operation. Tomorrow, if I can get us scheduled, I'll see about sewing up your wounds."

"Really?" That would mean an end to the painful scrapings and cuttings every day. Zeljka, Mihreta and Mima were as happy about this news as I was. They knew quite well what I had to go through each time my bandages were changed.

Tajib had another idea for keeping me busy. "Can you write now?" he said. "I'd like you to write something for the newspaper, a story about Suljo."

I told him I would do it.

The next morning, Dr. Gavrankapetanovic came into our room very early.

"Good news," he said. "Don't eat anything this morning, Jasmina, because you're getting surgery today. I'll close your wounds and maybe even do a little more reconstruction work on your legs."

In other times, in other places, people could expect to get nervous about having an operation but in Sarajevo, hearing that you were getting surgery made you feel lucky. The resources for surgery were scarce. With so little to go around, only the neediest could expect an operation.

An hour later, my doctor reappeared. "Here we go," he said. He put me in a wheelchair and we headed for the operating room in the hospital basement.

The operating room was a madhouse. It was full of wounded, some of them screaming or pleading. Blood was everywhere. Doctors and nurses rushed around madly.

One of the other doctors stood in front of my wheelchair. "She can't have an operation today. Look at what it's like down here!"

"When is it any better?" asked Dr. Gavrankapetanovic. "I've got to close her wounds. If I don't get her sewed up, her kidneys could fail."

The other doctor looked at me, then relented. They put me on the operating table and I watched as they prepared their instruments. All that gleaming steel made me nervous. I felt a little sick looking at the tools they'd use to cut me up. "Doctor," I said, "please put something on my belly to protect my baby."

"Don't worry, Jasmina," he said. "We'll take good care of you. How do you feel?"

"Scared."

"It's all for the good. You'll feel much better after this."

"Please give me the anesthesia now," I said.

They did and everything went black.

28

My Bosnian Soldier

I woke up back in my room. Tajib was holding my hand and all my friends were around me. I was happy to see them but I felt very sick and sleepy. My stomach ached and my head felt swollen and sore. My eyelids were heavy. I slept again.

When I woke up the second time, I felt much better. Tajib was still beside me, holding my hand.

"Coffee?" I asked him.

"Your mother-in-law is bringing coffee and food for you." Amra was there, too. I asked her to please change my underwear. "I feel so dirty."

"Sure," she said. Amra brought some water and washed my face and body. She was taking off my underwear when she suddenly stopped and looked up at me.

"Oh, Jasmina. I'm so sorry."

"What?" I said. "What is it?"

"Your period has started."

I felt that someone was ripping off my other arm. The baby had been my best reason to fight for my life. I wanted Suljo's child more than anything else in the world. The baby would be my one lasting reminder of the love Suljo and I had shared.

I looked at Tajib. I wanted to hear some words of encouragement or consolation from him but he felt as I felt. He put his head down and started to cry.

Dr. Gavrankapetanovic came in to check on me. He was smiling as he entered but then he looked around and saw what had happened. His smile disappeared. He sat beside me and took my hand.

"Jasmina," he said, "I lied to you. You lost the baby on the day of the explosion. The baby could not possibly have survived. You had severe internal hemorrhaging."

I turned my face to the pillow.

"I've known this all along," he said, "but I decided not to tell you. Listen. As a doctor, I have to be strong. I have to keep everyone's spirits up. But I'll tell you this—on the day they brought you to the operating room, I cried. You're so young to have lost so much. But I also knew that you had to keep fighting. I couldn't let you give up. And you haven't let me down, have you?"

I squeezed my eyes shut, trying to hold back tears. I shook my head.

"If you'd known that you'd lost the baby, too, you might have given up. You might have died. You might not have tried to walk again. Suljo would be so proud of you now. That's your gift to him. You will go on and you will live. That's what you'll do for him. One day, you'll have many children. Now take a deep breath."

I did as he said. His words were like a song to me. "Feel better?"

"Yes." But I was still fighting tears.

"That's my Jasmina," he said. "That's my Bosnian soldier."

I kept being strong until he had left the room. Then I put my head on Tajib's lap and cried for hours.

Suljo's family took it hard, too. That baby was all that any of us had left of Suljo.

Azem came to see me late that night. He was overseeing an offensive on the front line called Stup so he couldn't visit me very often anymore. The war was making Azem into a block of steel but the loss of the baby was very hard even on him. The last shred of my earlier life, my happy, normal life before the war, was now gone.

And the war went on.

It kept changing our lives and none of the changes were good. More and more wounded civilians and soldiers flooded into the hospital. There wasn't room for them. Patients had to be moved from one clinic to another in order to find the most efficient use of space. Zeljka, Mihreta and Mima were moved out of my room. Their injuries no longer required as much attention so they were sent to a clinic with fewer resources. Saying goodbye was hard. We had all gotten each other through so much.

"Jasmina, good luck," said the soldier, Mihreta. She was good at putting on a brave face. "We'll come visit you as soon as we can and then you'll come visit us."

"Good luck. I'll see you soon!"

They left and in their place came three new women. They were all older, in their thirties or forties. We didn't have much in common and I felt so alone. The hardest thing was waking up without my friends there. There had been a routine for the four of us. The first thing I would see in the morning was Zeljka's arm creeping out from under the sheets, groping for food. Her bed was next to mine and she always covered her head with a pillow so the first thing I saw was her arm and then her face. Mihreta was very loud. Her voice was the first thing I would hear, usually complaining about what the doctor was liable to do to her when he arrived for his morning visit. She hated the doctor's visits. As for Mima, her first concern was getting a cigarette. If she didn't have one stashed, she'd leave the room in search of one.

29

Glimmers of Hope

October 1992

That first morning without them, I missed all three terribly. Amela, the girl who brought breakfast to our room every day, noticed that I was sad.

"I can get a wheelchair," she said, "and I'll push you to see your friends. Their clinic is right across the courtyard from this one."

"Really? That's great! Thank you!"

She got me out of bed and into the wheelchair. Crossing the courtyard was the first time I'd been outside in over a month. The weather was beautiful—the sun was bright and warm on my face. I took a deep breath. Inside the clinic, there was always the smell of blood. The outside air was fresh and clean.

"Amela, isn't this beautiful? It reminds me of my life before the war. Summers in Visegrad with all my friends around me were the best time."

I remembered. But it was hard when remembering the good

times not to have the war memories intrude. When I thought of Visegrad, about the rivers and swimming and the cafés…when I thought about Suljo's smile and Samir playing soccer, I couldn't help but picture myself in a wheelchair with one arm and emptiness in the place of Suljo and Samir.

Many people had suffered worse than I had. That's what I reminded myself. No matter how bad things were, they were better than they could have been. And with the Serbs intent on ensuring our destruction every day, the natural trend was for things to get worse and worse. That's why we had to fight and struggle daily, to try and make the next day better.

I thought of Dr. Gavrankapetanovic who smiled even when his heart was heavy. He made us believe in ourselves even when he knew terrible secrets. So although I could not put Suljo and Samir out of my mind, I smiled as Amela wheeled me into the room with Zeljka, Mihreta and Mima.

They were surprised to see me so soon. I chatted with them for an hour and then I had to go back.

Days later, the arrival of more casualties meant another shift of patients. For me, it was a good thing. I was moved, too, and rejoined my three friends.

We improved a little bit every day. I took more and more steps with Tajib supporting me only a little. Mima started to walk without crutches. Mihreta could walk with only one crutch. Only Zeljka was still stuck in a wheelchair. She couldn't use crutches because she had lost five centimeters of bone in her arm and the doctors couldn't fix it, at least not yet. Normally, they could have done more for her. But not while the city was under siege and resources were stretched so thin. Surgery could only be justified when a patient needed it to save her life.

Zeljka needed to get out of Bosnia. So did I if I was ever going to really get my legs to work again. Katarina thought that maybe a hospital in America would sponsor us so that we could be flown there for treatment. Zeljka and I talked about America as our salvation, though we treated it more as a fantasy. We talked about how the American surgeons would fix us up. Then we'd go into business together, maybe open a boutique.

I didn't get my hopes up as much as Zeljka did. Bosnians, I knew from experience, could rely on help from Bosnians. The U.N. wouldn't even let us defend ourselves so what were the chances that Zeljka and I could actually end up in America?

Then one day, Katarina came into our room grinning so broadly that we were ready to believe the war was over. "I have excellent news!" she said.

"What? What?" Zeljka was sure she already knew what Katarina would say.

"Children's Hospital in Boston will take three patients for treatment. Zeljka, that's you, Jasmina and a sixteen-year-old boy who can't walk. If everything goes right, we'll all leave together in just a few days!"

Zeljka was ecstatic. "Really? Oh, Katarina, you've saved my life! Ha! We're going to America!" This had been her only wish and it was coming true.

I was happy, too, though I had mixed feelings about leaving my family. I hadn't seen my mother, little brothers or sister for a year and I hated the thought of leaving without seeing them one more time. On the other hand, I could do more for them outside of Bosnia. Once I had been treated, I could work and send them money and warm clothes from abroad.

"I have another piece of news," Katarina said, "one that I hope you'll be very happy about, Jasmina."

"Tell me!"

"I helped two journalists go to Megega and they brought food and medicine there. In a few days, they're going to come back to Sarajevo with videotapes of Megega and a view of Visegrad."

That was good news. Megega was a village on the banks of the Drina, only fifteen kilometers from Visegrad. It was the last village in the area that the Bosnian government still controlled. There were about two hundred Bosnian soldiers around Megega which wasn't much compared to the Yugoslav Army. But the Serbs still hadn't overrun the area. They were content, so far, with just keeping the village surrounded and cut off.

We knew that many refugees from Visegrad had fled to Megega. They were living witnesses to what the Serbs had done but we had no real contact with them. Megega was something of a mystery. Many of us from Visegrad hoped that some of our family had escaped to Megega but we didn't know for certain if they had.

As soon as Katarina had told me about the existence of these videotapes, I couldn't wait for them to be brought to Sarajevo. When Katarina finally got her hands on copies of the tapes and brought them to the hospital, we had no electricity. I had to keep waiting. Finally, Tajib came early one morning to wake me up. "We have electricity at the barracks," he said. "You can come watch the Megega videotapes with us." At the barracks, Bahe made a bed for me to lie on. All the soldiers were like brothers to me and they took good care of me while I was there.

When the first tape started, I wasn't so sure I wanted to see it after all.

Visegrad was completely different. All the Muslim villages around it had been burned to the ground. There was a parking lot in the center of the city where a mosque used to stand. You couldn't tell anything else had ever been there. Another mosque, one near my childhood home and on the banks of the Rzav, had been shelled to rubble. The city looked like a corpse.

Our sixteenth-century stone bridge, Na Drini Cuprija, had been partly destroyed. I couldn't understand that. Yes, the bridge had first been built during the Turkish Empire, but it was a heritage that belonged to all of us. It made about as much sense as blowing up America's Statue of Liberty because you didn't want anything French in your country.

The second tape featured interviews in Megega with survivors and witnesses from Visegrad. The first person on the tape was a woman of about thirty, who all of us watching the tape had known before. We didn't recognize her, however, until she said her name due to how badly her face was disfigured.

She was one of seventy-three people who had been herded into a house by the Serbs. After the people were inside, the Serbs used their own cars to block the doors shut. The Serbs then set the house on fire. They played loud recorded music to cover the victims' screams. The woman on the tape was the only survivor. Her family had all burned to death and she looked like something from a horror movie. Her hair had all been burned away. Her ears were shriveled and scarred and she had been burned so badly on one side that her arm looked as bad as my legs had first looked.

But she was impressive. She spoke with dignity, telling the story—without tears—of how she had survived.

Many more accounts followed hers. Each story was harder to listen to than the last but it began to sink in for me just how strong these people were. How do we survive the things that happen to us, these horrible things? By taking this moment and then the next one, one at a time. By telling our truth without being broken to pieces by the difference between what our lives once were and what they had become. Listening to these people, I found myself feeling stronger and stronger.

Our friend, Enko, leapt out of his chair. "Hey! That's my mother!"

We laughed and cheered, we were so happy for him. He hadn't known anything about the whereabouts of his parents until suddenly seeing his mother, alive and well, on tape. Amidst all that bleakness, this was a glimmer of hope.

Many more of us saw images of family members. Tajib, Azem and I saw one of our aunts and her children. Every now and then, someone else would shout when they recognized another face.

Watching the tape made me realize all the more how much I missed my mother.

The next morning, Ramo came to see me at the hospital. "The phone link between Visoko and Sarajevo has been fixed," he said. "Your mother called. She's waiting for you and Tajib to call her back. Here's the number."

I couldn't wait to hear my mother's voice. For three months, Visoko and Sarajevo had been connected only by radio.

The telephone for my ward was on the second floor of the clinic. There was no elevator. I still couldn't walk without Tajib holding me steady and using stairs was a distant dream.

But I yearned with my whole heart to hear the sound of my mother's voice and I didn't know how long I might have to wait for Tajib.

"What are you doing?" Mihreta asked as I struggled to get out of bed.

I grinned at her, "I'm going for a walk."

It would have been more accurate to say that I was "going for a shuffle." My feet didn't leave the floor and I had to stay next to the wall.

My roommates didn't try to stop me. I made it into the hallway and then to the stairs.

Now it was going to get hard, I thought.

The first stair was, in some ways, the most difficult. To get my foot up the six inches of that first obstacle, I had to bend my knee more than I had yet been able to. I bit my lip, held onto the railing and tried.

Pain shot through my leg but I kept bending my knee anyway, willing my foot to rise just a little farther, a little farther, just an inch more.

By the time I had negotiated that first step, my whole body was damp with sweat. I felt shaky but also victorious. After that first step, I knew I could manage the one after that.

I was soaking by the time I made it to the top. I shuffled the rest of the way to the phone. My hand shook as I dialed the number Ramo had given me.

When I heard her answer, my whole body started trembling and my tears flowed again. I was always crying. In my whole life, I had never cried as much as I did in the hospital.

At first, I didn't know what to say but then the words were rolling out of me. "Mama, Mama, how are you? Mama, I want to see you!"

"Jasmina, my dear daughter," she said.

I started sobbing like a baby but I didn't care. I wanted to feel her arms around me, easing all my pain. I needed her so much. She cried, too, and we had quite a conversation, each of us getting our words out in a rush between sobs.

"How did it happen?" she asked me, then asked more questions before I could answer the first. "Which arm did you lose? How are your legs? Can you walk?"

"Mama, I lost my right arm up to the shoulder. My legs are getting better. I've started to walk. Everything is getting better now. I want to see you so much but I might not be able to come to Visoko. I have to go to America with Katarina for more medical treatment."

It wasn't easy for either of us, the thought of my going away before I had seen her again. She knew that I needed better medical attention than I could get in Sarajevo but she wanted to see me, too.

Our call was too short. But it would not have been long enough, even if I had been able to stay on the line for hours. A phone conversation just couldn't take the place of being in the same room.

30

Disappointment, Tragedy & Resolve

A few days later, Katarina came with more news. This time, it was bad news.

"Even though Children's Hospital is willing to treat you," she said, "the U.N. doesn't consider any of you to be wounded enough for safe passage out of the country. They won't help you get out."

I was sad but Zeljka was devastated. "What do they mean, 'not wounded enough?'" She raised her useless arm. "I can't even walk with crutches. How wounded do they want me to be?"

I felt so bad for her. I had sensed all along that there would be a problem with any plan that depended on the U.N.

For my own part, I started to push myself harder and harder. If the U.N. was going to make me walk out of Sarajevo, that's what I'd do. I would find a way. So every day, I got out of my bed and walked as much as I could. I walked from our clinic to the orthopedic clinic to visit the nurses I knew there.

At the end of a second month, I was finally released from the hospital and went to stay with Suljo's family. I had to say goodbye to Zeljka, Mihreta and Mima. I bade Dr. Gavrankapetanovic, my second father, farewell. From that day on, I said goodbye a lot.

Katarina got pregnant and forty days into her pregnancy she decided to go back to America alone. It would be better for her baby. Azem, she hoped, would soon be able to follow her. My in-laws and I were having breakfast when Katarina and Azem came by so she could say goodbye to us.

Azem could have left with her, actually, but he didn't want to leave his country yet. Like others from Visegrad, he cherished the thought of going back there to fight for the city in which he was born.

Katarina was a sister to me now. I was very sorry to see her go. I think it was hard for her, too. She had wanted me and Zeljka and the wounded boy to be with her when she left.

Only a few days after that, Tajib came to Buca Potok to say goodbye. That was even harder on me. He'd been with me almost every day in the hospital. He'd held me steady as I learned to walk. He had scolded me into eating and staying alive.

But the Bosnian Army was managing to get soldiers out of besieged Sarajevo and into Central Bosnia and Gorazde. From there, Tajib and his friends were going to go to Megega and fight for Visegrad. That had been their dream. Tajib, especially, had wanted to go. We knew the concentration camp where my father was being held was close to Visegrad. Part of the plan was to try to capture Serb fighters who could be traded in a prisoner exchange for men being held in the camp. From what we heard, prisoners at the camp were frequently tortured and Tajib couldn't stand the thought of that happening to our father while he couldn't do anything to free him.

They went by way of Visoko and Tajib saw his five-month-old daughter for the first time. After a visit of a few days, he and the others went on to Megega.

December 10th, 1992 started out as a pretty routine day. My wounds were still bandaged and I had to go every so often to the hospital to get my dressings changed. Azem's driver, Fadil, came to Buca Potok to take me to the hospital, as he had done on several other days. After the nurse had changed my dressings, Fadil took me to the Marshall Tito barracks so I could visit Azem. When I got there, a soldier outside of Azem's office told me, "He isn't here. Azem left a message for you, though. He wants you to go to his apartment."

What was he doing there? Fadil always brought me to the barracks after the hospital. If Azem had wanted to change plans, why didn't he tell his driver about it?

Fadil drove me to the apartment. When I knocked on the door, Suada answered. I hadn't seen her in a long time. She still lived in the building across from Azem's.

"Suada, hi! What are you doing here?"

"I came to wash the dishes. You know how men are. They never notice the dishes until there's a big pile of them. Come in and sit down. Azem and Ibrahim should be here any minute." She was right. We didn't have to wait long for my brother and his friend. Three other men were with them. Azem introduced the strangers as Dr. Sokolovic and two friends from another brigade.

Ibrahim came and sat next to me. Azem sat on my other side. Everyone was very quiet and somber. It wasn't like Ibrahim or my brother to be that way. I studied their faces and they looked back at me without saying anything. I wanted to ask them what was going on but I was afraid to.

Azem threw his arms around me. This was going to be big

news. Azem never hugged me without a reason. I thought he was going to tell me that he, too, was going to go to Megega to fight alongside Tajib and the others. I'd been expecting that. He'd know that it would be hard for me to remain in Sarajevo without anyone from my own family.

He broke the silence. "Jasmina, Tajib is dead."

I screamed.

At the top of my lungs, I screamed. I squeezed my eyes shut but no tears came. I didn't have any left to cry.

When would the dying end? When would I stop losing brothers?

Azem held me tightly. He held me by the shoulders and looked into my face. When I started to calm down, he turned to the doctor. "It's all right," he said. "You can go." He'd been afraid that I might need some sort of medical attention when I heard the news.

"Jasmina," Azem said, "can you write something about Tajib? We want to put it in the newspaper."

When he asked me that, I remembered how Tajib had asked me to do the same thing for Suljo. I started to scream again. Azem and Ibrahim hugged me and we all began wailing with grief. It helped. The sound of our crying helped push the pain from inside of us.

When I could finally manage to speak, I said to Azem, "When did it happen? Is he the only one who died?"

Jasmina's brother, Tajib

Tajib had died on December 4th in a firefight. The two sides were fighting very close to each other and Tajib had tried to get into position to take a Chetnik prisoner. He wanted so badly to capture a man he could trade with the Chetniks for our father.

But he had been shot in the neck and stomach.

As far as Azem knew, he was the only casualty from his group. We didn't know at the time that Enko and Buba had been with him and were missing. It was days later that Bosnian soldiers in Megega found their bodies. Many men died near Megega.

Soon after that, Suljo's cousin, Nihad, was another casualty. He was killed on Zuc Hill and left behind a wife who was three months pregnant.

New Year's Eve 1992 was a somber night for me. In Bosnia, December 31st had always been one of our big celebrations but 1992 had brought me so many losses. With my friends, new and old, I tried to put a good face on things and celebrate anyway. But it was hard. The fourth of January was coming—it would have been my first wedding anniversary with Suljo. And life was no better in Sarajevo. The Serbs grew more bold in their defiance of the U.N.

Azem was leaving Sarajevo to go to Mount Igman. After that, he was planning to go to Megega. I was staying behind with Suljo's family. Without Azem around, I would miss my mother that much more. I dreamed of seeing her. I dreamed of seeing my younger brothers and sister.

"People leave Sarajevo all the time," I told Azem. "I can get out."

"Be realistic," he said. "It's not easy to get out. And it's dangerous. Able-bodied people die trying to escape."

I didn't argue with him about it. But I had made up my mind.

I was going to visit my mother and then I was going to America. Whatever the obstacles, I would find a way over, through or around them.

The Serbs would have to kill me to keep me in Sarajevo.

Jasmina shortly before attempting to escape

31

Escape from Sarajevo

December 1992 – January 1993

One of the first obstacles to getting myself out of Sarajevo was convincing other people I could do it. Azem continued to say that I should be realistic about the difficulties. I could barely walk, much less run. And hurrying across open ground on foot under the Serb guns was the only way out. No matter how much I believed I could manage to do it, my self-confidence wasn't enough. The one escape route—through U.N.-controlled territory at the Sarajevo airport—was unfamiliar ground. I had to go with someone who knew the way, someone who believed that I could do it.

Azem's duties called him out of Sarajevo. Of my big family, I was the only one still trapped in the city. That fed my determination, especially after my friend Ramo went to Gorazde. On his way back to Sarajevo, he picked up a letter from my mother. I savored every word.

"Our Dear Jasmina, we're now all sitting together, what is

left of our family, and we wish you could be here with us. Azem
says it's impossible for you to come but I hope that in better days
we will be able to see you..."

Reading those words, I could hear a voice deep inside me
saying, *Try, Jasmina. Try to get out. You'll make it.*

Being separated from my family was the thing that drove me
most. Yes, I wanted to go to America for proper treatment of my
wounds. But the thing that truly mattered was getting to Central
Bosnia to see my mother.

Fortunately, my mother-in-law shared my longing to get out
of Sarajevo to see her own family—she and her brother had been
separated for a long time. And she believed in me. If others
could get out of Sarajevo, so could I. We would go together.

My father-in-law knew some women who regularly crossed
through the no man's land of the Sarajevo airport to get milk
from Central Bosnia for their children. It was never an easy
journey. The escape route through the U.N.-controlled airport
was flanked on both sides by Serb strongholds. At the far end
of the corridor were deep trenches filled with barbed wire. The
U.N. patrolled the passage in their armored vehicles and shined
lights wherever they saw activity. The goal of the U.N., for
reasons still unclear to me, was to keep the victims of the siege
in Sarajevo. If they caught you crossing their corridor, they
searched you for weapons then loaded you into their vehicles
and took you back to the city.

The worst part of the U.N. policy was their business of
shining lights on people. When the Serbs on either side of the
corridor saw the illuminated Bosnians trying to escape, they shot
at them.

One of the women who regularly made the crossing said that
she would take us when the time was right. My mother-in-law
and I had to be ready to go on short notice.

While waiting for the signal, I lived my life one day at a time, keeping busy visiting friends in the hospital. By then, Zeljka had been in the hospital for five months. One day, I arranged for her to have a short visit with me and my in-laws.

As Senad drove me and Zeljka home from the hospital, Zeljka stared at the streets of Sarajevo. The city's condition was even more shocking for her. I had seen the destruction happening day-by-day since before I was wounded but she was emerging for the first time to see the city where she had grown up reduced to rubble. Almost every building was heavily damaged. Her first trip out of the hospital should have been a joyous occasion but it wasn't.

Nonetheless, she made the best of things. She talked about how wonderful it was to get out of the hospital for a while. I wished that I could do more for her, that I could bring her with us when we left Sarajevo. But she couldn't get around without a wheelchair. For her, the trip across the airport would be impossible.

During Zeljka's visit, my father-in-law brought the news: the time was right. Our guide had sent word for me and my mother-in-law to get ready. We would meet her the next morning and prepare for the crossing the following night.

"That's wonderful!" Zeljka said. "Jasmina, have the best of everything! I know you'll get across the airport and see your mother. Please call me. Don't forget me."

"Of course I won't forget you, my sister!" I told her. "Not ever. We went through a lot together at the hospital. And we have good times ahead. You stay strong and I'll see you one day in America. Remember that business we're going to start."

I knew it was going to be hard on her to be left behind. I still found it hard to believe that the U.N. wouldn't help her to get out of the city for promised treatment in the United States.

The next day, Senad took me and my mother-in-law on a circuitous trip to Dobrinja, the district of Sarajevo that was very close to the airport. Part of the area was in the hands of the Bosnian Army but the Serbs controlled the rest. Dobrinja was the jumping off place, the link to the parts of Bosnia that were still relatively unscarred by the war.

There were other farewells to say and that's why I say our route was circuitous. Senad went with my mother-in-law and me as we accepted the good wishes of Emir, Malja and Ramo. We told them to take good care of themselves. Then we said goodbye to Suljo's grandmother who couldn't believe I was serious about walking across the airport. "You really mean to go? Really?" Then to my mother-in-law, "Mevla, is she serious?"

I suppose it did seem like a crazy idea. My legs were still very stiff and though my balance was better, I still shuffled along rather than striding. But I told everyone that I would manage. I had to.

When we finally got to Dobrinja, our guide-to-be, Abia, just asked if I was up to the journey. When I said that I was, she took me at my word.

Abia was about thirty years old and had two small children. She was in charge of getting food for her kids, parents, sister-in-law and husband, who was a soldier. She looked like a very strong woman and I was confident that she'd get us through safely.

But her first words were disappointing. "I know you want to go tonight," she said, "but my friends and I have decided to try tomorrow night instead. You're welcome to sleep here. In any case, it's getting late. It's a good idea to have a look at the situation in the daylight so that you'll know your way around a little better in the darkness."

I'd been both nervous and excited about making the crossing that night so the delay was frustrating. Abia's family was very nice, however. They made us feel at home right away and I soon felt better about the wait. Abia was right that it would be better for me to see the territory I would have to cross.

"How many of us will go tomorrow?" I asked her.

"Three other women, the two of you and me. But there's something I must explain to you. Those of us who make this journey take a sort of pledge. We agree not to look after each other. It's the only way. You have to run fast to get across. If you fall, no one can come back and help you. We won't wait for you and you aren't to wait for us. I know it sounds hard-hearted but to do it any other way invites trouble. If the U.N. catches one of us, the others have a chance to make it if they keep going. Understand?"

We said we understood. I was worried, though, because if I fell, I might not be able to get back up with only one arm and legs that wouldn't bend.

"If the lights shine on you," Abia continued, "you have to crouch down. Remember that you're hiding from both the U.N. and the Serbs. You can carry only one bag. Don't overburden yourselves. You have to be fast. Do you agree to all this?"

"Yes."

"All right."

We were up late that night listening to more of her advice. In the morning, she took me to a doctor in Dobrinja to change my bandages and check my wounds. Then she took us within sight of the airport.

"Those are the transports that will try to stop us," she said.

There were eight of the armored vehicles.

"They move back and forth all the time but every once in a while some will be clustered on your left and some on your right, so there will be a gap of open ground before you. That's when you run. Never forget that both sides of the corridor are held by the Serbs. If you stray just a little to the left or the right, you'll walk right into their hands. You have to go straight."

I had heard stories about people who had tried to get across the corridor but had been captured by the Serbs. Terrible things were done to them, according to those reports, but the truth was that no one knew for certain what became of such people. They disappeared.

Watching the U.N. vehicles patrol in the daylight, I couldn't see how anyone successfully crossed so much open ground. But the women I was going to escape with had already made this journey many times.

It was winter, the end of January, 1993. A light snow sifted down. The night was quiet. No one was on the streets. In the distance, we could hear the usual gunfire and explosions. But other than that, the only sound was our footsteps. The six of us came to the building next to the airport. We looked across to the other side, toward the black void that was our goal. Somewhere out there were the wire-filled trenches. Beyond that, the rest of the world.

The far ground that I couldn't see in the darkness was the beginning of refuge, the beginning of a normal life. On many nights before this one, other Bosnians had stood where I now stood, looking into Central Bosnia. From there, one could flee to Croatia and from Croatia, one might manage to go anywhere in Europe.

How many attempting the crossing had been stopped by the U.N. and brought back to Dobrinja? People would just try to cross again. And how many, on their second or third attempt, were killed by Serb shells or snipers?

I was afraid. My heart was pounding. It was impossible not

to think of all those people who had died attempting what I was about to attempt. I was a little sad, too, to be leaving Sarajevo because there had been such an intensity to life there. The good times with Suljo, Tajib and my friends had been desperately good times. Sarajevo was the place of my strongest joys, terrors and sorrows. I was about to leave all that. And I was leaving behind Zeljka, among other friends.

"Are you ready?"

I nodded to Abia. So did the other women.

"Jasmina, Mevla, you stay close to us. I don't want you getting lost. Remember, go straight ahead. Be quiet and run fast!"

I took a deep breath. We could hear the crack of rifles now and then.

"All right," said Abia. "Let's go."

As soon as we stepped away from the buildings, I knew I was in trouble. The earth was soft and wet with snow. It felt like land that had just been tilled for planting. It would be hard for anyone to run on such soft ground, but for me...

My boots sank deep and with each step I struggled to lift them.

"Jasmina, come on! Hurry up!"

I fell. I heard a bullet zip overhead. It was too dark for the snipers to have seen us but from time to time they fired blindly into the corridor.

I couldn't get up. I pushed myself out of the mud with my one arm, but my feet couldn't get any purchase in the soft ground. Then my mother-in-law and Abia were next to me. Abia pulled me to my feet. She was indeed a strong woman.

The other three women were somewhere in the darkness well ahead of us now.

"Hurry!"

I put one foot in front of the other hoping for solid ground somewhere ahead. But everywhere the earth was just as soft and wet. I made it a short distance before falling again. This time, painfully, I made my knees bend just enough to get back onto my feet.

Another bullet zipped over our heads. Some distant shots popped like firecrackers. I reminded myself that not all of the gunshots I heard were from snipers shooting into the airport. There was always gunfire in the night around Sarajevo and much of it was being fired into other parts of the city. If they couldn't see us, they most likely couldn't hit us.

I was grateful for the darkness but I was also afraid of losing my way. Fortunately, I could still hear Abia and my mother-in-law moving ahead of me. From time to time, they stopped to wait for me.

I'm going to get out, I reminded myself. *I'll be in Central Bosnia soon.*

Again I fell. Again Abia came to my side and lifted me out of the mud.

She never suggested that I should turn back.

"Is she all right?" whispered someone. I made out four figures in the darkness—my mother-in-law and three others. That was when I realized that the other three women had waited for us. I was worried now that we'd all be caught because of me.

"I'm all right!" I whispered. "Go!"

I guessed that we were nearing the halfway point.

Once again, I fell. I clenched my teeth, angry and frustrated. Abia was coming back for me but I got to my feet on my own.

Suddenly, the ground around us was lit up.

"Crouch down!" Abia warned, squatting. "It's an illumination flare!" The U.N. had fired the flare high over our heads and it drifted slowly down on its little parachute. I wished for a gust of wind that would carry it away from us.

I couldn't crouch because of my wounds. My knees were still too stiff so I just pitched myself face-forward into the mud.

The light revealed another group next to ours, five or six other people who were trying to get out of Sarajevo. One of them said, "Stay still. Maybe they'll catch someone else and we'll be able to run for it while the U.N. is busy with them." That sounded like a good plan but suddenly there was a much brighter light shining on us. A U.N. transport rolled up close, its light pinning us to the ground. The U.N. soldiers said something to us but I couldn't understand them. "Shit," said our new friend. "We almost made it. Put your hands up and don't move suddenly. They're pointing their guns at us."

In the bright light, I couldn't at first see that this was so. But some of the U.N. troops got down among us and they were indeed pointing guns at us.

"Don't worry. They're afraid we're armed. Keep your hands up until they've lined us up and searched us."

She was right. The U.N. soldiers lined us up and searched us. Then they loaded us into the transport for the drive back to Dobrinja. In the lights, I could see how afraid my mother-in-law looked. I could also see how thoroughly mud-covered I had become.

I knew one line of English, a phrase Katarina had taught Zeljka and me in Kosevo Hospital. Even though I thought the U.N. were French, I figured they knew English, so I tried my sentence.

"Please let me go, I lost my arm, I need a better hospital."

I might just as well have asked in Serbo-Croatian. They ignored me.

Before an hour had gone by, we had been released and were back at our starting point, looking again across the open ground of the airport.

"Ready?" Abia asked.

We started out again. I was more confident from having gotten used a bit to moving over the wet ground. I was determined not to fall.

But I fell. As many times as in our first attempt, my feet slipped in the cold mud. And whenever Abia helped me up, I tried to go faster to make up for lost time which only meant that I fell more often.

"Go on! Go on!" I said. As before, everyone else was staying behind with me. *What about the promise that we wouldn't look after one another? If something happened to one of these women because I slowed them down, I would feel terrible for the rest of my life.*

Every time I fell, though, Abia was waiting beside me. It saved time if she didn't have to backtrack. As we rose together from the mud for the eighth or ninth time, we heard one more sniper bullet—a close one, I thought.

I heard the rumble of U.N. transports behind us. Light played over the corridor again. I looked back, afraid, but this time it was someone else pinned in the glare. We were almost across and the U.N. was busy with someone else. For now, anyway.

We slowed down a little and I didn't fall. The remaining obstacle was the three ditches filled with barbed wire. I slid into the first ditch feet first. It wasn't too deep, though the coils of wire were very thick.

As we started to negotiate the wire, I could see why a daytime crossing would have been impossible even without the interference of the U.N. The barbs snagged my clothes and my skin. In the process of freeing my leg, my arm would get hung up. If I freed my arm, my other shoulder would be painfully scraped and snagged. If the Serbs had been able to see us, we'd have made perfect targets. They could have corrected their missed shots at their leisure.

Picture how insect-eating plants use an insect's struggles to draw it deeper and deeper into the trap—that's how the barbed wire was for me. Soon, I had wire tangled around my legs and pinning the sleeve of my jacket. I struggled so hard that some of my old wounds opened but I still couldn't free myself.

"Abia!" I called. She came back to me and looked me over, feeling to find how the wire tangled me where she couldn't see. Then she told me how to move while she pulled the strands of barbed wire this way and that. My clothes tore. In other places, my clothes stuck to me from the blood and mud.

But it didn't hurt. The only thought in my mind was fear of the U.N., that their flares would light us up for a Serb sniper or that their vehicles would come to the far end of the corridor when we were within sight of our goal and take us back.

Scraped, jabbed and bleeding, I got through the second ditch on my own. It was just a matter of taking my time and moving very slowly so I could stop as soon as I felt a jab or a snag.

The last ditch, however, was a big problem. It was two meters deep. Jumping in and getting through the wire was the easy part. The real struggle would come when I tried to get up the two-meter wall of mud on the other side.

I decided not to worry about it until the moment came. Taking things one obstacle at a time had brought me this far. That, and the help of the women who had taken a pledge, no matter what, not to help me.

I actually felt happy jumping into the last ditch. We were at the far edge of the airport and the U.N. vehicles were cut off by the two ditches we had already crossed. I had almost done that which practically no one believed I could do.

I had almost walked out of Sarajevo.

There was a lot of wire in that last ditch but I had figured out how to take my time moving through it. Inch-by-inch, snag-by-snag, I negotiated my way. I heard the whispers of my mother-in-law and other companions on the far side of the ditch. Abia was a silhouette against the gray sky when I cleared the last of the wire and looked up.

The wall of the last ditch was so cold and slippery, it was like trying to climb up a wall of wet potter's clay—a wall that was well over my head.

"Come on, Jasmina. Give me your hand."

I reached for her. She took my hand and pulled but my knees still would not bend much. I wriggled at the end of her arm like a hooked fish but I couldn't gain any purchase to help her. Strong as she was, Abia wasn't strong enough to pull me up. My face was in the mud and all our efforts did was rub me around in it.

For a moment, my feeling of helplessness was like something from a bad dream. I had made it across the airport, avoiding the U.N. while praying that the snipers shooting into the dark wouldn't get lucky then worked my way patiently through three sets of barbed wire...but I was going to be stuck on the threshold of freedom because with my one arm and stiffened legs, I couldn't clamber out of a ditch. A stupid ditch.

It wasn't fair, to come so far, to be so close...

"I'll push," said one of the other women from above. She slid back into the ditch beside me, put her hands under my feet and lifted. Abia pulled and fell backwards with me. I landed facedown on the ground and Abia and my mother-in-law helped me stand. Then Abia helped the other woman out of the ditch.

I was a mess of blood mixed with mud. There was mud all over my face and grit in my teeth. But I couldn't stop smiling. I thought about what Azem would say when he saw me. He'd been sure that I could no more walk out of Sarajevo than I could sprout wings and fly out. And my mother! I'd soon see my mother and all the rest of my family! We walked toward the first buildings of Butmir, the Bosnian-held village at the end of the airport.

"We need to get her cleaned up," one of the women said. "Maybe someone in Butmir-"

"No," I told her. "My brother is on Mt. Igman. I can wait until we find him. He'll have someone look after me."

"Then this is where we part company," said Abia. "Jasmina, Mevla, the soldiers here can help you find Jasmina's brother. Good luck."

"Thank you for everything," said my mother-in-law.

"Good luck to you on your way back to Dobrinja!" I said.

32

"Okay. Go ahead."

January – February 1993

I was happy that the trip went only one way for me. Incredibly, soon after these women met the people who sold them food, they would make the return trip before dawn.

I tried to spit the grit out of my mouth. It was hard to walk—my legs were stiffening up worse than ever. Suljo's mother and I looked for a doctor. I figured I could wait for medical attention but a doctor was likely to have a car and might drive us to Mt. Igman where Azem was. We asked around in Butmir and someone finally took us to a doctor.

"Hey, you look like you've had a mud bath!" the doctor said when he opened his door to us. "Are you wearing clothes under all that dirt?" His smile and jokes reminded me of my surgeon. "Let me see your wounds." He had to clean away some of the mud to look me over.

My mother-in-law was muddy, too, but not like me. I looked like a creature made of clay. While the doctor examined me, I explained what what we really needed was a ride. "My brother is an officer on Igman. He'll take care of me if we can just get in touch with him. Or maybe you can call him? I know he'd send a car for us."

"Do you know exactly where he is?"

"On Mt. Igman, that's all I know."

"Then it's impossible. Igman is a big mountain with many Bosnian soldiers. I'll get you a ride to Hrasnica and maybe somebody there will be able to find your brother."

Hrasnica was a village right under Mount Igman. We got there at about one in the morning and the village was dark and silent. Most of the houses were just ruins and no one was on the street. It was snowing and shells were coming down nearby. The doctor left us with the Bosnian Police but they couldn't do anything more for us. "Stay here until the sun comes up," they said. "Someone can drive you up to the mountain in the morning."

But we didn't want to wait. We were sure we could find someone who was going to Igman that night. Surely there was some military traffic going that way. So we left the police station and kept walking through the village streets. But Hrasnica's streets were empty. We were tired and cold and wet. We sat on the side of the street to talk about what to do. Maybe we should have stayed in the police station, after all.

Two boys came walking down the dark street. "Excuse me," I said. "We just came from Sarajevo. We want to go up on Igman. I have a brother there. Do you know anybody who can take us?"

"Nobody's going there now," said one boy. "But early in the morning, trucks take Bosnian soldiers up onto Igman and civilians can ride along." Then he said, "You look like you could use a place to rest and warm up. Why don't you come to my house? My sister and aunt will wash your clothes and feed you."

"Thank you," I said, "but just look at how muddy we are. We can't ask you to-"

"Don't worry. There's nothing to feel uncomfortable about. You won't be the first people to come to our house from Sarajevo looking like this."

We were shivering and admitted that it really would be good to get out of our wet clothes.

"Come on," the boy urged. "My aunt and sister will be happy to help. And in the morning my sister can go with you to Igman."

We followed him. His house was right at the foot of Mount Igman. His aunt, cousin and sister helped us out of our muddy clothes and took them away to wash them. They let us clean up, then gave us some of their own clothes to wear until ours were clean and dry. They fed us and called another doctor to come check my wounds.

They didn't even know us but while we got a couple hours of sleep, they stayed up late to finish cleaning and drying our clothes. The boy's aunt woke us. "Time to catch the trucks to Igman!" she said as she brought us our clothes.

"Thank you! You've been so kind to us!" we replied. But we didn't have enough words to express how incredibly grateful we were.

The boy's sister took us to a place to wait for the military trucks. There were a lot of people waiting and trucks were going to different parts of the mountain. We ended up on a truck going to Pazaric.

Pazaric would take us closer to Visoko—it was on the far side of Igman. Visoko was, after all, our final destination, the place where our families were. But I was afraid we'd miss Azem by going that way.

Still, I was excited. In Pazaric, we would be only two hours from Visoko. We could hitchhike. Soon, I would be with my family and my mother would know how to contact Azem. I'd get to see him eventually.

Getting to Pazaric was like entering another world. Stores were open and they had food on their shelves. We could hear gunfire in the hills but compared to Sarajevo, it was nothing. My mother-in-law and I were looking around feasting our eyes when I saw a man I knew sitting at the wheel of his car. "Hey, Mama! Look! That's Muriz from Visegrad. He can drive us to Visoko!"

"You're right," she said. "It's him."

We hurried across the street as I shouted, "Muriz! Am I ever glad to see you!"

He looked at me and there was no sign of recognition in his face.

"Muriz, don't you know me? I'm Jasmina, Azem's sister." I could see the emotions cross his face. He recognized me and was clearly sad to see what had become of me but still managed to smile.

"Jasmina, how are you? How did you get here? I thought you were in Sarajevo! Azem was telling me about you just this morning. He's in a meeting right now with Commander Buljubasic and I'm waiting for him. I'm supposed to drive him to visit your family after the meeting."

It was perfect. We couldn't have had better luck.

"I've got some candy here in the car. Come on, get in. How long has it been since you ate some candy?"

We didn't have to wait long for Azem to come out of his meeting. He and Commander Buljubasic came striding toward the car. Muriz said, "Put your heads down!" Then he jumped out. "Azem, I've got something for you in the car. I hope you like it."

When Muriz opened the door of the car, Azem opened his mouth but no words came out. Then he laughed. We all laughed.

"Jasmina! Mevla! How did you get here?"

"We walked across the airport," I told him. "And now we're going with you to Visoko!"

Azem's smile vanished. "Well, we might not get through. The Croatians have blockaded the roads."

"The Croatians? Why? They're our allies."

"They should be our allies. But since the U.N. hasn't done anything serious to discourage the Serbs, it's getting to be every man for himself. Since the Serbs have taken some of Croatia, the Croatians figure they need to grab some of Bosnia."

"That's crazy!"

"It is and we're hoping that cooler heads will prevail. Not every Croatian commander thinks that the way to beat the Serbs is to act like them. Meanwhile, we're stuck in Pazaric. There's no way for us to get to Visoko at the moment. Some of my men are garrisoned in a school. The two of you can stay there until the blockade is lifted."

"I guess we don't have much choice," I said. My hope of seeing my mother that day faded away.

The school Azem was using was in the middle of the woods and it was nice to breathe fresh air after Sarajevo. The soldiers—they were just boys—were good company. Mevla and I stayed with them after Azem and Commander Buljubasic went to Gorazde with a food convoy and to bring back women and children to the relative safety and comfort of Pazaric.

We had a long wait. Day after day, the Croatian blockade remained in place. On January 28th, I celebrated my 20th birthday in the woods.

Then one day, one of Azem's friends showed up with a car. "Mevla! Jasmina! Get your things! The Croatians have opened the road but they could close it again at any time. Hurry!"

We'd been there for ten days, just two hours away from my

mother all that time. It was a great relief to be going and I said a grateful prayer.

"Do you know the house where my family lives?" I asked our driver.

"Don't worry. I've been there."

We passed the first Croatian checkpoint without trouble and made good progress before reaching the second one. There, all the Croatian soldiers standing around made me think of our escape from Gorazde and the Chetniks who had stopped us on the outskirts of Rogatica. I was afraid. But this time, I wasn't fearing for my life. Instead, I was worried that they wouldn't let us through, that I'd get so close to my mother only to have to turn back.

I thought my fears would be realized for sure when I heard the soldier tell the driver of the car ahead of us, "This road is closed!" The soldiers made that driver turn around.

The soldiers approached our car next.

"Where are you going?" said the man in charge.

There was fear in our driver's voice as he replied, "We're going to the hospital in Zenica. This girl is wounded!"

The soldier leaned into the car and looked at me. I felt my face get hot. I didn't have to act at all in order to look scared.

He said to the driver, "What do you have in back?"

"Milk for the children. That's it."

The soldier went back to look then said, "Okay. Go ahead." I had never heard three words more beautiful than those.

Visoko was gorgeous. The sun was shining and birds were singing. In my heart, it felt like spring in the middle of winter. People on the streets were smiling. Children were playing and no one was shooting at them.

Tears of happiness welled up in my eyes. The war was still going on but here it seemed very far away.

"Jasmina, can we go first to my brother's house?" asked my mother-in-law. "Then the driver can take you to your mother."

I couldn't say no. Her brother, Nihad's father, shared a sad bond with her now. They had each lost a son to this war. "Sure," I said, "we can go there first."

Her brother was in front of his house as we pulled up. I hadn't seen Suljo's aunt and uncle in some time. They were good people but I didn't want to visit long. I was finally so close to seeing my mother that I couldn't stand any more delays. I hugged everyone and asked the driver to take me to my mother's house.

I knew it was the place before the driver stopped because my Aunt Zema was in the yard. I recognized her even though her hair was white and she was so thin. Her hair had always been a beautiful reddish brown. But that was before the war.

She was busy tidying up the yard and didn't notice us—she had always been a little hard of hearing—so she didn't know I was there until she saw me running toward her.

"Jasmina!" she cried, giving me a hug. Then she ran to the house. "Naza, Naza, Naza! Mina is here! Mina is here!"

My mother, brothers, sister, aunts, uncles and cousins came running out. My sister-in-law came out carrying Tajib's daughter. I was so happy. I was afraid that I would wake up and it would all turn out to be a dream. I wanted to cry. I wanted to laugh. Everyone wanted to hug me and I didn't know who to embrace first. I wanted to hug and kiss all of them at once.

"My daughter, I was afraid I'd never see you again!"

"I missed you, Mama. I missed all of you terribly."

"Everyone told me you couldn't possibly come!"

"When I read your letter, I had to come. I had to see you."

I kept feeling for a long time that it must all be a dream. It felt so strange to have my wish come true, to be among my family again.

It really sunk in for me the next morning at breakfast, that I had finally returned to a normal life. My big, noisy family was all around me. We had lost Samir and Tajib and my father was still missing, but we had Dalila, Tajib's daughter, who was now six months old. Her smile was some compensation for the loss of my brothers. She was the future.

In Visoko, I went to the cafés with my sister, Amira and many of my old friends from Visegrad. My mother made us all of the dishes for dinner that she had made before the war. No one had to wait in line for water. There was water all the time—all you had to do was turn the tap. There was electricity, too.

No one shot at us. Day after day, no one tried to kill us. I felt like I had spent a long dark time at the bottom of a river, unsure of which way was up, unsure of how to get back to the air and the light. At last, I had seen a glimmer and I had made my way. Lungs bursting, I had made my way. I was patient, in spite of everything. And now I was breathing again and the sun was shining down and the sky was as blue as blue could be.

I was home.

Epilogue: The Rest Of Our Lives

The reunion with my family in Visoko was the end of one journey and the beginning of another.

There were many obstacles still to overcome in my efforts to reach America and Boston Children's Hospital where I could have the surgery I needed and be fitted with a prosthesis.

Some of these obstacles were frustrating, though none of them were anything like the danger of escaping across the airport. My experiences had taught me patience and courage—useful traits when it came to dealing with the ever-changing rules of bureaucrats and international refugee policies.

At the border with Croatia, a border guard ordered women with children and pregnant women off the bus. They weren't allowed safe passage through Croatia—only childless adults under sixty could get visas. For a few minutes, these women and their children stood with their bags at the side of the road, stranded, while the frustrated bus driver couldn't decide whether to proceed with those who were allowed or turn around and take the rejected refugees back to a Bosnian town. In the end, we took them back, then tried to cross with everyone at a different checkpoint. But the rules were enforced in the same way everywhere. Finally, the women with children were left at a

Bosnian Army barracks. The rest of us slept in the unheated bus. We were finally permitted to pass the next morning. When I later reached Katarina on the phone, she told me it was Valentine's Day, February 14th.

I had to cross other borders illegally. No one wanted to accept refugees, even temporarily. Friends of friends smuggled me from Croatia to Austria so I could say goodbye to Suljo's sister. I wanted to go to Germany from there since I could stay with my sister, Mukadesa, so a truck driver who she knew risked his job by smuggling me from Austria to Germany. He hid me behind the cab of the truck as we went through the border checkpoint. When he told me I could come out, I cheered. He laughed and said, "Most people would be nervous about doing something like this. Weren't you scared?"

"German border guards aren't Chetniks," I told him. "What's the worst that could happen to me?"

I had been more concerned about getting him in trouble with his employer but he said the risk was worth it. People should help each other.

At the American consulate in Frankfurt, they rejected my visa application because my documents from Boston Children's Hospital were too old. It was almost funny. I had escaped life-threatening bullets only to find myself under fire from bureaucrats. While I stayed with Mukadesa, I wrote to the United Nations office in Bonn. I told them my story and asked for help. A few days later, we received a letter from a man named Walter Brill, pledging the support of his U.N. office. The letter informed me about an organization in Frankfurt called Raphaels-Werk that could assist me with my visa application.

Unfortunately, the people at Raphaels-Werk said that new legislation in the U.S. required that I wait in Germany for another six months before I could be admitted to America as a refugee. Katarina had been working on my behalf in the U.S., though, and a few days later she managed to secure helpful letters from Senators Joe Biden and John Kerry. In all, I spent two months waiting in Germany until I finally flew to Boston on a free first-class ticket generously provided by Swissair.

After that, good news followed good news.

I had my surgery and I got a prosthesis which I am still learning to use.

A month after my arrival, I found myself in a Boston maternity ward helping Katarina as she gave birth to Azem's baby. Azem was still in Bosnia but we were able to get a telephone connection through to him. He was listening in, four thousand miles away, as his daughter took her first breath and began to cry.

Six months later, Azem joined us in America.

Months after that, my third niece came into the world when Mukadesa gave birth in Germany.

And then a year later, my father was finally released from the concentration camp and rejoined my mother in Visoko. Sadly, he had been tortured. (More on that in a moment.)

Zeljka was eventually allowed to leave Sarajevo and she went to New York for the surgery that freed her from the wheelchair. She has since visited me in Boston.

For a few years, the river of our lives ran salty and bitter. Or another way to think of it is to say that we were swept along through dangerous rapids. The two men I loved most in the world, Tajib and Suljo, both died. The current held all of us down on the river bottom for a long time and not all of us were permitted to rise again to the light.

But the calm after a rapids is sometimes the sweetest and brightest water. There is so much in my life that I am happy about now. My English is getting better every day. After my first six months of school, I won third prize in an essay contest by writing about "What Learning English Means to Me." When peace returns to Bosnia, I hope to go back and teach English.

I never thought I'd fall in love again after I lost Suljo but day-by-day, life renews us. In Boston, I met Enes, a refugee from a small Bosnian town and we began dating. The doctors told me that I can still have children.

I feel like the whole world is mine. I have good friends in America, people who have helped me to get settled here. I go out with friends, study, play games and listen to birds singing in the morning.

In Boston, no artillery shells fall on the city. No enemy lurks on the edge of the city trying to grind the life out of us. Children don't have to worry about snipers.

The river runs salt, runs sweet. It is very sweet, the river I find myself in now.

But even my happiness itself keeps me from forgetting. When I look out my apartment window and see children playing, I can't help but think of the children who played on my street in Visegrad. I think of the August soccer and swimming competitions at the Sports Center. As I write this, in 1994, there is still no peace in Bosnia. It will come, but it has not come yet.

The lessons of my life are things people have heard before. But it's one thing to hear the lessons and another to really live them.

No matter what happens to us, no matter how bad things look, there is always the next thing to do, the next step to take. Tiny steps took me from my hospital bed in Sarajevo, across the airport, into Germany and here to America.

"All you can do," I have heard people say, "is all you can do." But that's all that you're required to do—just the next thing that you can.

Another thing I learned was something that I thought I already knew. My mother said it to the father of little Bojan, the boy whose body my brothers brought out of the Drina.

"We're here to help each other."

The people who helped me are so numerous. Some of them were powerful and important men like U.S. Senators. Some were not much different from your most ordinary neighbors, like the truck driver in Germany, Abia, the woman who helped me across the airport corridor, and the many people who opened their hearts and homes to refugees, to strangers.

There is a saying that I've heard in America. "God helps those who help themselves." God tells us the same thing in the Koran: "Help yourself and I will help you." So even though it is true that the generosity of strangers sustained me, it took my own efforts, too. God and all those helpful strangers could only meet me halfway. I had to take the first step.

Finally, I learned some things about wounds and how they heal. Operation by operation, surgeons have done reconstructive work on my legs. Bit by bit, they work better. With time, they are healing.

It didn't happen overnight.

Wounds to the heart do not heal overnight, either. Some people have asked me about forgiveness. When will I be able to forgive the Serbs?

I lost so much. I lost two brothers I loved dearly. I was still a newlywed when I lost my husband, unborn baby, right arm and the strength of my legs in the mortar attack.

I am angry. In some ways, forgiveness is the wrong thing to ask me about because I think it's better to speak instead of justice and healing.

Do I want revenge? No. I also don't want war crimes to go unpunished. To do nothing about rape camps and the massacre of helpless prisoners invites more of such crimes in other places in the future. The certainty of eventual punishment may deter such acts in other wars. Certainly not punishing such acts is a great risk. We must not dwell on the past but we must protect the future. There must be justice without revenge.

And there must be healing. There must be, between one person and the next, true peace. I take my father as my example.

He was brutally tortured in the Chetnik concentration camps. All of his teeth were removed. I don't know the details—he won't speak about them. He says that we must pay less attention to our past and more attention to our lives now.

Part of our lives now is remembering to see other human beings one person at a time. We're here to help each other—not just the people who are like us but the people who we find at our doorstep in need, whoever they are.

If we do that, in bitter times or sweet times, then we are healing our own hearts and also the world's. We are living the life I once lived in Visegrad where we did not first ask someone in need, "But are you Muslim? Are you a Serb?"

In my lifetime, I may never again see Visegrad as it once was. But it lives in my heart, the place where I grew up with some friends who shared my religion and some who did not. Like the far end of the Sarajevo airport, it is a destination that I want very much to reach.

I can't know beforehand every step of the way there. I don't know what obstacles others will need to help me with or who those others will be. But I will take the first step as it presents itself to me. And then the next. And the next. I may be turned back but I will try again.

One step at a time, our feet will find the way.

Jasmina Dervisevic

Boston, Massachusetts
1994

Jasmina with her daughter, Leila, husband, Enes, and son, Alem, near Boston in 2013

Afterword by Randy Larsen

It's been four years since Joany Lebach insisted I read the first edition of Jasmina's book. It sat on my desk for several months until one day, when needing a short break from my office, I took it outside to a park bench thinking I would read the first chapter. I read the entire book in one sitting.

My first thought was, "What can I do to help take this remarkable story to a larger audience?" The next week, I flew to Boston to meet Jasmina. Two months later, I returned to hear her speak to an overflow audience in an auditorium at Tufts University. Following that, I told my friend and business partner, Jay Lavender, that he had to read her book and we needed to bring her story to the screen.

I am no stranger to warfare: I flew 400 missions as a teenage helicopter pilot in Vietnam, studied war and conflict for more than four decades, and served as a professor and department chair at the National War College in Washington DC. Nevertheless, the more I got to know Jasmina and her story, the more I realized how little I knew about warfare from the perspective of the innocent.

It was the innocent who paid the greatest price in Bosnia. More than half of the four million residents in Bosnia became refugees, an estimated 100,000 people were killed and 20,000-50,000 women were raped, many of them repeatedly. I will never forget the moment I first read Jasmina's description of what it was like to be denied support from NATO. The Bosnians didn't ask for NATO or UN troops—just the means to defend themselves from genocide so they didn't have to fight tanks with old hunting rifles.

It was as if the world had come upon a rape victim while the crime was in progress and tied her hands so that she wouldn't do something violent to the rapist.

There are many who have endured the suffering Jasmina experienced as a young woman, but survival is our most basic instinct. What sets her apart is that in the midst of genocide, her humanity survived.

Since sharing our first cup of coffee in 2010, I have cherished my time getting to know Jasmina and learning how she spent the past 20 years—she became an American citizen, got remarried, started a family, built a successful career as an entrepreneur and motivational speaker, and continued to reach out and help those who are rebuilding her homeland.

But that's a story for another day…

Col Randy Larsen, USAF (Ret.)
Austin, Texas
July 2014

About the Author

In May 1993, twenty-year-old Jasmina Dervisevic escaped the genocide and arrived in Boston as the first Bosnian refugee granted permission to seek medical care in America. She had lost her husband, two brothers, uncle, grandmother and countless friends, as well as her right arm.

Over twenty years later, Jasmina still calls the Boston area home. She has a degree in business administration, runs her own real estate company and is a licensed insurance agent. A happily remarried mother of two children, Jasmina is a frequent guest speaker at schools and community events where she shares the remarkable story of her memoir, *The River Runs Salt, Runs Sweet.*

To hire Jasmina to speak, for other inquiries or to send correspondence, please email Jasmina@NSPYR.com.

Photo Credits

1. Visegrad photo courtesy of Jasmina Dervisevic-Cesic
2. Jasmina & Suljo walking photo courtesy of Jasmina Dervisevic-Cesic
3. Dijana, Selma & Jasmina photo courtesy of Jasmina Dervisevic-Cesic
4. Katarina & Azem photo courtesy of Jasmina Dervisevic-Cesic
5. Samir photo courtesy of Jasmina Dervisevic-Cesic
6. Jasmina & Suljo seated photo courtesy of Jasmina Dervisevic-Cesic
7. Tajib photo courtesy of Jasmina Dervisevic-Cesic
8. Jasmina injured photo courtesy of Jasmina Dervisevic-Cesic
9. Jasmina, Leila, Enes & Alem photo by Dickie Morris

For more information about Jasmina, *The River Runs Salt, Runs Sweet,* NSPYR and updates on upcoming books & projects, sign up for our email list by emailing Fans@NSPYR.com as well as like, check & follow:

NSPYR.com
twitter.com/NSPYR
facebook.com/FueledByNSPYR

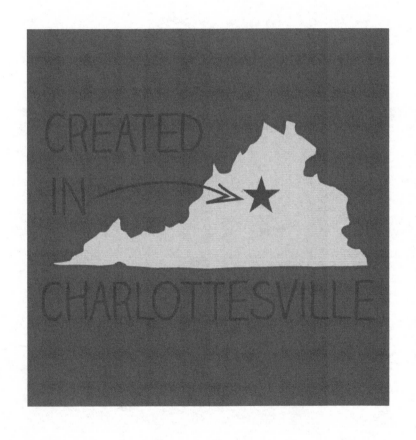